STEPNEY
CALLING

THOUGHTS FOR
OUR DAY

Other books by Jim Thompson:

Half Way: Reflections in Middle Life (Fount, 1986)

The Lord's Song (Fount, 1990)

CONTRIBUTOR TO:
Trevor Huddleston (OUP, 1989)

STEPNEY CALLING

THOUGHTS FOR OUR DAY

JIM THOMPSON
BISHOP OF STEPNEY

EDITED BY
PAUL HANDLEY

MOWBRAY

Mowbray
A Cassell imprint
Villiers House, 41/47 Strand,
London WC2N 5JE, England

First published 1991

British Library Cataloguing in Publication Data
Thompson, Jim
  Stepney calling: thoughts for our day.
  1. Christian life—Devotional works
  I. Title   II. Handley, Paul
  242

ISBN 0-264-67208-9

Extracts from *Half Way* are used by
permission of the publishers, Collins

Typeset by Cambridge Composing (UK) Ltd

Printed and bound in Great Britain by
Biddles Ltd, Guildford and King's Lynn

CONTENTS

INTRODUCTION

'I always listen to you in my bath', 'We always hear you sitting up in bed having our cup of tea', 'We never miss—even if we have to listen in the car on the way to church'. I don't know how many hundreds of times people have said these rather awe-inspiring words. As I sit before the microphone looking at its spongey impersonal presence I imagine a thousand steaming baths with radios perched behind the taps, rows of bedrooms, breakfast tables, cars where my disembodied voice is heard talking about God. The strength of the situation is that people can turn off if they don't want to go on listening and they have total control. In a strange way this makes both the listener and the broadcaster free to communicate.

For me broadcasting—whether on radio or television—gives an opportunity which I find demanding but precious. It's not so much the chance to talk to millions of people, though that is important to someone who passionately believes in the message committed to him, but it's more the level of engagement with the listener. This is why I prefer radio to television because I think that it is altogether a 'hotter' medium—that is the people listening participate in the broadcast in a much more vivid way than when their minds are distracted by watching us speak under the pressure of the lights, with the sweat on the upper lip and all the personal distractions, like where on my head is the little hair I have left arranged? Or when we did the first 'take' were my legs crossed? Was my pectoral cross there or here? The level of engagement is proved by the letters I receive. People take the trouble to write and express their ideas, their anger, their disagreement, their thanks and their enjoyment. A 'Thought for the Day' I gave on midlife gave rise to a huge correspondence, to an article and in the end to my first book. So there is constant feedback and people say far more to me than I do to them.

Whether I am reading a script over which I have laboured long till late at night, or whether I'm being interviewed on some difficult topic, I'm always aware of the self-exposure involved. I'm only too aware that people see right through

1

broadcasters and hear in a range of ways whether we are speaking our truth or no. Some politicians seem to think that people don't see what they say as betrayed by their attitude, their tone of voice, their body language. Perhaps if I was in their position I would accept more compromises with the truth. If I am aware that I am being questioned on a matter which raises passions in the Church and in society, I take care to say what I have to say in a way that will convince as many people as I can. It's useless to frighten people away from thinking into an unnecessary pre-judged and hostile reaction. But I retain a strong sense of responsibility that I must search for the truth and try to speak it.

To try and speak the truth is not just about ideas and facts outside myself, but it is also 'my' truth. It is the truth which emerges from me, from my experience, from my history, from my personality. It is not like reading the news or like journalists striving to be objective (if they are), but it is a communication of the whole person. Sometimes people say 'he's so human'. I'm not sure what that means—because I've been human since I was conceived and I hope I will be human when, by the love of Jesus, I come to be with God in heaven. 'He's so human' must relate to the belief that bishops or priests are not normally human. Obviously wearing strange clothes, being treated with too much respect, being liturgically at the point of the pyramid offering worship to God could well give us strange notions about ourselves, but most priests and bishops remain rooted in the ordinary. I suppose 'he's so human' is a recognition of vulnerability, that is: 'he feels the same things we feel', 'he's not afraid to express the mess he's in', and above all 'he finds life funny as we do'. Rabbi Lionel Blue gives us a deep assurance because we can see his holiness that he cannot see through his offering of himself—warts, twinkles and all.

So, in one sense, the broadcast is inevitably not just the message but also the person who gives it. The medium is the message, said McLuhan, and it's that fact that puts the person in the hot seat. I rarely do an interview without feeling stained in some way because I've not answered the questions well, or I've let down people who trusted me, or I've damaged a cause I care about by not thinking clearly enough, or wasted the excellent answer which only occurred to me on the way home. But whatever the situation, it is a self-exposure, and especially when the subject of the message is God.

As every preacher knows, or should know, to preach about God is a risky business. The temptations are grievous especially in the area of claiming to know more than we do, of trying to make the trumpet sound with a certain note when inside we are full of doubt, or of teaching others to do what we have found impossible, or speaking from behind a mask . . . so many temptations. For someone who broadcsts about God, the dangers multiply because of the public nature of the utterance. There are the political tightropes, the pit of banality, the 'relevance' cul-de-sac, the slough of sentimentality, the jokes that didn't work, the restricted throat, the bored interviewer and so on and so on. God is viewed in a million different ways and many of them are a precious passion to the believer, so there are many spiritual corns 'out there' to be trodden on. But above all this, there is costly necessity for truthfulness in faith, hope and love. In the middle of conflict and argument this can be severely tested. We make a joke about 'sincerity' on *Good Morning Sunday*, but the joke is a release from the anxiety that the medium will take us over and exclude God from the communication as well as dilute our integrity in the cause of entertainment.

So this exposure often brings me back to fundamental questions—Who am I? Who have I become? Who should I become? How is it with God and me? It is for this reason—that the person is, in part, the message—that it seems right to tell something of my own story, as a background to this selection of broadcasts and talks, so that you may put together the speaker and the message.

In some ways it would be natural to begin with my birth in Harborne, Birmingham, in 1936, but I think the more important moment in my own journey was a sort of rebirth which took place when I was 20 in the churchyard of St Mary's, Charlton Kings, near our home in Cheltenham.

It was on Christmas Eve in the late fifties. I was training to be a chartered accountant. My fellow articled clerks and friends were celebrating at the pub when one of them said 'we must go to church'. I was horrified, being a bit the worse for drink and being a practising unbeliever. After school I lost what little faith I had, and although I argued more than most about God I had no sense of Him—I regarded myself at best as an agnostic. We set off for church on this frost-cold night and the service had already begun. Looking back on it now, as a bishop, when I see

3

the slightly, or very, inebriate arrive late for Midnight Mass I remember again that night. I refused to go into church with my friends, and stayed outside sitting on an ancient grave stone. This had a distinctly sobering effect and as I began to look at the amazingly clear starlit sky I began to examine my life. Then I had a sense of God telling me that, in spite of all my failures and sins, He loved me and He was encouraging me to search for Him. I remember getting on my bike and riding home singing because I sensed that I was free and that a new life was opening up for me. It is important to me not to overstate what happened that night but I regard it as the great turning-point of my life for which God, through the process of my mess and anger, doubt and failure, love and hope, was preparing me. It is especially important for the broadcasting because my calling came outside the Church. Although I love the Church even in all its fragmentation, I have always felt that my vocation was to non-Church people, like my parents and most of my friends and colleagues, and many of my relatives, who had so much good in them and whom, I believe, God loves, even though they did not find Church a real possibility. As I studied theology and learnt a bit about the faith through my experiences of God I began to see how important this speaking beyond the walls of the church to the world must be. It took me right to the heart of the Gospel of John and those wonderful words—which would have been read from the lectern inside the church on that Christmas night whilst He found me outside.

> In the beginning was the Word, and the Word was with God, and the Word was God. He was with God in the beginning. Through him all things were made; without him nothing was made that has been made. In him was life, and that life was the light of men. The light shines in the darkness, but the darkness has not understood it. *John* 1.1–5

So the Logos, the Word of God, is that energy and love of God through whom all created things have their being. There is a light in everyone to whom we can appeal. I do not regard myself as speaking to a 'godless' world, but a world filled with God, inhabited by people who know without knowing, who see without seeing—people like me. So the purpose of the broadcast about God is to put people on God alert, to remove secular cataracts from our eyes, to whisper in people's souls, perhaps even to 're-Christianize' folk religion. We are not trying to 'introduce' God to the world or to the human race, we are trying to uncover—reveal—God in our everyday experience because we breathe, love, laugh, in Him. Lionel Blue helps us to see God in the most ordinary events, experience and feelings because for him the universe is 'engodded'. It does not need a burning bush or angels in heaven, but as Jesus proved over and over again God can be found in a farmer sowing the seed, in a tree giving good fruit, in a man who stopped to help the victim of a mugger. So broadcasting about God is mining in human experience for the gold seam which is the precious love and truth of God.

It was not just the start to my Christian life which gave me a sense of urgency in telling people about Christ, but I can also trace other major interests reflected in my broadcasts which go back to early personal experience. For instance I return often to the plights and rights of minorities in our society. I identify with people who are misused by the majority. I have tried to trace this to its root and I think it is to do with being the fat boy. I could tell many stories of the fat Thompson—like being discussed by the rest of the boys in biology as to whether I would survive longer than them if we were shipwrecked in the Atlantic—or being used as a comfortable punch bag and being the endless butt of other people's jokes, or going on 'runs' at school and being a mile behind the others, hardly getting my feet off the ground, suffering through the whole distance; but more personal damage was done in my own attempts to divert attention away from me on to others. So as I grew up I knew a great deal of fear and though I completed exams successfully I felt inferior. It took me long years to struggle out of the 'fat boy' mentality and it was not until I had grown tall, and, more important, recovered some self-respect in the army that I began to see myself as I was. I realize now that there are many groups of people who have had to deal with being different, being misused by majorities, and indeed being harrassed and bullied for it. Jews, black people, gay people, disabled people, ugly people, very small people, people of different faiths, people of different race and culture. My own sense of being a persecuted minority was part of what made Jesus such a winner for me. I was Zacchaeus up a tree, a leper, a cripple, a sinner and yet he searched me out and accepted and loved me. No one I can remember ever asked me how it felt to be fat, it was usually used as a weapon against me, and how often this happens to minorities in any society. I would go so far as to say that you can tell how 'Christian' a democracy is by the way it treats its minorities. As I write this, I feel we are facing in Europe a dangerous time for minorities in the face of nationalism and a punitive streak in the corporate character of society.

Another theme in the meditations which constantly recurs is the attempt to demonstrate the credibility of God. This is the branch of theology called 'apologetics'. It seems to me to be of spectacular importance because of the massive and overwhelming tide of secular materialism. I can trace this concern, too, back to earlier events in my life. There was first of all the way I eventually came to faith, arguing late into the night, trying to seize hold of the truth and then in the middle of this struggle it seized hold of me. Then when I went to Cambridge to read theology it was a voyage of discovery which I found thrilling. I was reading for my degree in the sixties, that apparently despised decade, and I was learning to test out and articulate the faith I had discovered. We were encouraged to think! I remember a course of lectures given to the University by the theologians called 'Objections to Christian Belief'—historical, psychological, philosophical and intellectual objections. There was a sense that we could face any question and put any issue to God and, like Job, challenge Him to give an answer. *Honest to God* was written in these years and it demonstrated what Tillich called 'The Shaking of the Foundations'. We were subjected to famous German theologians who cast severe doubt on the truthfulness and historical accuracy of large chunks of the New Testament. I'm thankful to say I was never convinced because it seemed to me they always underestimated the memory and recall of the eyewitnesses and especially the disciples on whose evidence the Gospels were based. But it was as though we were being called into a new era where the three-decker universe was no longer believable, where the God who intervened by miracle and supernatural events in history was dead and we were encouraged to see in secular man the human race 'come of age', self-reliant, a friend of God no longer trapped in slavish dependence. I remember sitting at the Cambridge University cricket ground reading Bonhoeffer's *Letters and Papers from Prison* and being transported. Time stopped still and the power of his words written as he served his sentence before execution thrilled me and gave my faith a new coherence. He asked us to see God in the suffering of the people with him in prison—'the

God who is with us is the God who forsakes us'. But I was lucky to have the chance to read his other great works and I began to see that this faith in life-embracing Christianity was not to get rid of the 'otherness'—the transcendence of God—but rather to lead us to prayer, precisely to the God and Father of our Lord Jesus Christ.

But Auschwitz, Buchenwald and Belsen scarred the human psyche so deeply, and the terrors and waste of two world wars made people question whether there could possibly be an almighty God who was also loving. I think for many the question was shelved in the recesses of the mind and God in heaven became unreal and, in a way, unthinkable. Those of us who believed were seen as peculiar, swimming helplessly against the tide.

Two particular examples of this feeling of the credibility gap about God are especially relevant at this point. My first tele-vision programme in 1968 was called *New to the Job*. They filmed my ordination and then came back a year later to film how I was getting on as a curate in East Ham. I remember driving my battered old Hillman Minx down the Barking Road with a cameraman in the passenger seat and the interviewer asking me, 'Jim, is God here?' It was pouring with rain and East Ham's long roads and streets with their thousands of houses seemed to close me in and God out. As the question was asked the front tyre burst, and so I had time to prepare my answer— which was not unaffected I suspect by the burst! But the question was the question of the day—'Is God here?'—and it expressed the mood of the age. It expected the answer 'no' or at best 'probably not'.

If it needed confirmation in experience, there was my first Good Friday—arguably the most important day in the Christian year. Crowds and crowds of people walked along the Barking Road, to watch West Ham, and a small gathering of under twenty people sat in the vast church of St Bartholomew and listened to the new curate do his first Good Friday meditation. For many years in ministry in London I and my colleagues have battled against this vast secular tide like small corks in the rapids. So we have been battling all the time with unbelief—at funerals, at weddings, in people's depression, in people's cele-brations, in people's strengths and people's weaknesses. I have often felt like the court jester, a clown who everybody thinks is rather odd for keeping on about a King who is dead. Science appeared to describe the way things were and left no space for God—or so people thought. The pursuit of material well-being consumed the consumers and left little room or energy for spiritual growth and adventure. Perhaps above all we could find no convincing way of justifying God in the face of the evil and suffering in the world. It was a little like being a politician who has lost the trust of the electorate.

As I have tried to express this secular contemporary imprisonment in our skull, I have found that it has closed the minds of many people to the possibility of heaven and eternity. I believe that this undermines the whole sense of Godhead. Even if heaven is not 'up there' it is where and how God is. So we need to find new pictures of this dimension of God and many of my broadcasts have been aimed to restore a sense of paradise. But there is a yet more formidable obstacle to belief becoming more widespread. I'm not at all sure it can be overcome by argument as Job's friends discovered. On *Thought for the Day*, *Pause for Thought* and *Good Morning Sunday* we are often subject to the disasters which plague the earth. So many times I have been sitting content at 11.00 p.m. with my script for the morning ready and the phone goes and there has been a Lockerbie, a Hillsborough, an earthquake or a flood, a war or the death of some much loved public figure. So we are struggling in the early hours to give comfort, to express somehow the grief and to try to give some clues as to how God is not destroyed by it. Sometimes the tragedy has been caused by human error or wickedness, such as a terrorist bomb, sometimes there has been human inefficiency and carelessness so that by the next morning people are already looking for the culprits, but many of the disasters are natural and the obvious question follows 'Why does God allow it?' This apologetics is the same task as the priest or the doctor or the nurse has in trying to give some interpretation to parents of a child dying of leukaemia, but it is also so public and the broadcaster cannot convey comfort in any other way than words and feelings. It can help that Christ suffered as an innocent but it cannot be produced like the neat answer to an equation. We have to work against the idea that the natural disaster is something God has done and chosen to do as a sort of punishment and convey the truth that God is in the suffering, that this was what God was doing in Christ when he was crucified. I don't think, this side of heaven, there is any answer except faith. It is to give birth to faith, to stimulate, encourage and nurture faith that we try to build a way of looking at our own suffering and the suffering of the world, in the light of Christ. 'Faith gives substance to our hope and makes us certain of realities we do not see.'

The Bishop of Durham has created, almost singlehanded, an atmosphere of debate and interest in the great doctrines of our faith, the Incarnation and the Resurrection. Although many people have been hurt and infuriated, it has given many opportunities to bishops, clergy and lay people to talk about our beliefs. His way of tackling the issues has sometimes given offence but there is no doubt that to the secular twentieth-century mind he asks real questions. My own preference is to explore the faith of the gospel writers and move from *their* experience of mystery, wonder and amazement to discover the mystery, wonder and amazement which resides in God for *us*. It is certainly easier for me than it is for the Bishop of Durham, because I believe that the gospel records are much closer to the apostles and to Mary than perhaps he does. I always treasure that remark made by F. D. Maurice: 'Theologians are so often right in what they affirm and wrong in what they deny'. So I want to affirm, find parables, re-express the wonder of resurrection, so that it becomes real for us children of the twentieth century. This is, I am sure, what the Bishop of Durham wants too, but the stories he doubts are so vivid and profound and telling, and the alternative he gives seems abstract and intellectual, however passionately expressed. I believe we need him, but I hope we can move to a richer reconstruction. It is certainly true that it is the concrete story, the human experiences, life's jokes and pains which provide the sharpest means of communicating God.

Another recurring feature of the broadcasts is their political implications. A senior official at the BBC said to me that most of the contributions to *Thought for the Day* were left-wing. It is sad when people in such responsible positions accept the stereotypes created by the press. It's certainly not true that the contributors are uniform in their political beliefs, and the vast majority, most of the time, try to keep party politics out of what is 'protected time'. Because no one has a chance to answer back, it is important not to misuse the slot for party propaganda. Indeed, scripts are read beforehand by producers to ensure that this does not happen. In a way this is a parable of the argument about religion and politics which has been raging over the last decade. It is not, however, a new debate, but an argument thrown up by almost every decade. It is the task of the Church to try and identify God's will for individuals and for society. It is impossible to keep religious belief and political implications apart. The main reasons why the broadcasts attend to the issues of justice in society are first that many of us live and work in the front line where injustice is rampant, and, secondly, the Old Testament and the gospel constantly remind us that God's righteousness demands it.

Very few days pass when I am not confronted by some unfairness which most of our nation would reject if they knew enough about it. All we can do is describe our situation with as much objectivity as we can, offer the hope, and the gospel of God and His justice, and leave people to draw their own political conclusions.

My own political beliefs have gone through many changes. My first 'political' memory is of election time at my public school. We used to have the score up on the blackboards and a great cheer went up when the announcer said 'Conservative' elected. That was the assumption of most of the boys and their parents and I used to regard as oddities friends or relatives who didn't support the Conservatives. In 1966, however, I went to work in East Ham and I began to see a very different side of the world, to feel the effects of bad housing, unemployment and degrading environment. Compared with my own lovely home in Cheltenham, many of the people I met and tried to serve were living on impossible estates, with multiple difficulties. Then we went to live in Thamesmead as council tenants, in a concrete maisonette on the end of a balcony in the new town and became involved in all the teething troubles and angst of the birthpangs of a new community. It seemed impossible to prevent the planning mistakes that were so obvious to the residents' eyes. We would say at the Development Group of a new design for a linear block of flats, 'It looks like Gestapo headquarters! Build that and you will cause many people to become depressed and even mentally ill'—they did build it and people did get depressed. I began to realize that so many things which affected people's lives at the deepest level, such as their environment, their education, their health, their work, were in the hands of politicians and boards of directors. The corporate decisions affected individuals and often for the worse. Labour tended to be the people on the ground where we were and they identified with us. But then with the move to Stepney the level of problems which confronted us were enormously greater, and I had only had time to learn a little about the area when Mrs Thatcher was elected. Then have followed eleven years of tumult, through a massive rise and fall in unemployment, together with a new realism about the competitive world in which we have to make our way. There has been a welcome spread of home ownership to break up the monotonous council estates, but a disastrous increase in homelessness. A proper discipline about public expenditure has been accompanied by a sense that the surgeon is now cutting off the limbs on which society stands. Alongside the desire for greater accountability, there has been the abolition of the strategic authority for London and the Inner London Education Authority. Now the boroughs are everything and there seems to be little co-ordination in the capital city, leaving many of its schools with serious problems, its transport increasingly snarled up and its quality of life undermined for many of the most powerless in the community. So power became the key issue in the 1980s and it has been exercised with ruthlessness, in the certainty of those who possessed it that they were right about everything. Where I work I am aware of how the people who are 'done to' feel as they experience society passing them by. I am convinced that we need efficiency, we need creative individual effort, corporate enterprise and thriving economic institutions, and we need to earn the money to create the sort of society we want. Into this turmoil, and as a symbol of it all, came Canary Wharf and the question whether we were to welcome it as the renewal of Docklands, the provider of a hundred thousand jobs and a new and vibrant extension to the city, or whether we were to question it as a modern Tower of Babel built basically on rampant materialism and dedicated to endless growth which could only be achieved by continuing the outrageous imbalance between the affluent First World and the other two-thirds. These are big questions. I have tried to write and speak about them to find some sort of Christian view, give some hopeful interpretations, but market forces still seem such a maverick god. I sometimes wonder if generations to come will address Prince Charles's question to the architects of Canary Wharf when they claimed it would demonstrate above all 'confidence' . . . 'Confidence in what?'

After my first years in Stepney I concluded that I would

belong to no one in terms of political parties. The *Independent* newspaper ran an advertisement which expressed my own politics—'Independent "it is"'—'well I am'. So I try to pursue the manifesto of the Kingdom of God and attend to the issues with the best briefing I can, and try to bring to bear a biblical vision to inform my own reactions. Quite often it has been that independence which is useful to other people and indeed I believe it is pretty essential for a bishop who tries to give leadership in the Church where there are people of every political persuasion. It has seemed important to me that I should use my broadcasting opportunities to be a voice for those who are never heard. I do not believe that any party has all the answers and certainly I have never found a party manifesto I can agree with throughout. But those who criticize us for talking about God and political issues in the same three minutes should go and read their bibles day by day and they will see that to pray and study the scriptures leads immediately to implications about corporate realities as well as the salvation of individual souls.

The last and the most important theme is that of prayer. It is not easy to talk about because so much of it happens in a secret place. As Jesus said,

> When you fast, anoint your head and wash your face, so that men may not see you fasting, but only your Father who is in the secret place. *Matthew* 6.17–18

A broadcast is hardly a 'secret place'. But it is important to break through the common view that people have of themselves that they don't pray. My father knelt by his bedside every night but no one knew except my mother. There are so many prayers that people do not recognize as prayer: 'Why should this happen to me?', 'O God help me', 'Oh God I'm sorry', 'I'll do anything if you'll make it all right', 'God, I can't stand any more', 'God it's good to be alive . . .'. These basic human responses betray our parentage. As St Paul says, our inarticulate groans, the fact that we can say 'Abba Father', demonstrate that God's Spirit is joined to our spirit. But for each of us it is a very personal journey. I have tried to understand my own and find it difficult, so it's no wonder if it's hard to describe the road for other people. I don't know when I first was aware that I was praying. We did not pray 'publicly' in our home and so, as a child, I was not used to prayer outside school. At school there were always prayers in the morning and in the evening. I went to chapel with everyone else and was earnest about my confirmation, but looking back on all those years it does not look to me like prayer. I went through the act because we all did, but even when I read a lesson, or led prayers, it was more important to me that I did not make a fool of myself, and I listened intently to my own voice rather than meaning the words or loving God. I never thought God was real and personal and concerned about the passions of my life—its fear, its joy, its hurt, its fun, its urgency. God was at best an idea, abstracted from myself. My deepest feelings in chapel were only embarrassment, discomfort in my suit, the agony of not coughing and the music, but as for some encounter, some conversation with God, not at all. I played at it because everyone else did. It's no wonder that this flimsy edifice crumbled when I left the conformity of school to go into a world which hardly mentioned God at all, except as an expletive. My school prayers had given me the official language of prayer, had taught me the great songs of faith, but it was a façade.

I began to pray in earnest around the time of my experience in the churchyard. I had been asking the question 'Is anyone there?' because I had such a need and I had received in the thoughts and feelings an intimation that God was there and listening. From then on I prayed, or what I think of as prayer, a great deal of the time. It was more like a battle with an unknown stranger God. I was to sing a hymn much later which exactly expressed it, 'Come Thou traveller unknown . . .', and Jacob's encounter and wrestling match with the stranger at night also gave me a parable of the experience. It seemed to me the most important fact of life. If God was there then to converse with God, to love God, to hear God was the most precious fact of my life. I suppose I fell in love with God and went through many of the same sort of extremes of feeling and non-feeling of height–depth as falling in love was to bring me later. So much of my prayer is self-centred, trying to be God-centred and other people-centred. But the energy is grown first in the battle with myself. So my sins, my failures, constantly send me to my knees. Maybe they are too important in my eyes, but they seem so directly to come between me and God. I remember the first time I realized I was forgiven and accepted, I was caught up into the heaven of feeling thankful and alive from my toes to my head. Then through the years, as I experienced the suffering of others, not only individuals but communities and even nations, the prayers for other people became important. As I worked in the inner cities I found so many places of prayer with the brave, faithful, joyful and suffering people with whom I worked. I also found exaltation in nature which became so vivid by contrast with East London. So my inner thoughts, struggles, hopes, fears, joys became a sort of continuous intercourse with God—not in a holy way, but as it were blood, sweat, tears, grief, laughter, etc., etc., etc. As a bishop I have tried to learn to pray the prayers of the Church so that liturgy, public prayer and my broadcasting are owned by the inner self and are true to the person I am. It is still a matter of amazement that God seems to stick with me in His wonderful grace and forgiveness.

I have tried to lay bare some of the roots of the self who looks at the microphone and hopes to enter that place we yearn for where there can be real communication between me and thee and God.

It just remains for me to thank especially the *Today* team, Brian, Sue, Peter and John for always making 'Big Jim' feel so much at home; to thank Roger Royle who I know is loved by many people and with whom I have so enjoyed *Good Morning Sunday*, and to Derek Jameson who, like me, shares an affection for East London, and represents in some ways the contemporary British agnosticism. I also have to remember the people who produce the 'Thoughts' who have the courage to say to me at 10 p.m. that a script written for the morning in the turmoil of my life is no good . . . in the nicest possible way and have made sure that for every thousand thoughts there are ten thousand in the waste-paper basket. Thanks too to my successive secretaries who through the years have deciphered my scrawl and encouraged me to go on, and most to Sally, my wife who accepts the late-to-bed early-to-rise formula with anxiety, waiting on the alarm clock.

Faith–no sedative

Faith is not a solution to life, it is a way of living it. Faith does not free us from perplexity, or even our share of the agony, it rather affirms the meaning of our life and, through the struggle, gives us some assurance of God with us in the middle of all that mess. Faith does not by-pass human destiny, it opens wider and offers us abundant life. Abundant life does not mean trouble-free, painless, anodyne life, it means life lived to the full, sharing its mysteries, its agony and its beauty. So when we search for the clues of faith, we are not likely to find large doses of serenity (though I hope we shall find some); we shall find the inner courage and love necessary to face the future in the way Christ would have us travel. **Half Way**

At the edge of a mystery

In his autobiography, Arthur Miller describes a childhood visit to the synagogue with his great-grandfather. At one point in the worship, the old man took off his shoes to reveal naked white feet. He then made Arthur cover his eyes and forbade him to look. Then began a thumping and a bumping and deep voices all singing their own individual song. In the end the boy *had* to peep—and there was the unbelievable sight of his great-grandfather and the other old men having a wonderful time singing and dancing before the Lord. He quickly shut his eyes again, but the effect on him was profound. He had been at the edge of a mystery which was sacred and puzzling.

Reading this of the young Arthur Miller I was reminded of generations of Russians who have kept their sense of mystery and God alive, because their grandmothers had secret icons in their bedrooms, where flickering candles lit up the haunting holy face of Christ or his mother.

Looking back on my own childhood, I don't remember ever being given a sense of mystery. Everything had to be explained.

Perhaps, without realizing, I met the great God when I

climbed the rocks or watched a stag cross a combe. But no one helped me glimpse the sacredness at the heart of our life. Religion was portrayed as something we learn about, not a God to encounter.

I was thinking this was not just my story, but the story of many of us in post-war Britain. Maybe the faculty for mystery died somewhere. Perhaps that accounts for the appeal of Africa and India, because the sense of the sacred is so alive there. School Chapel, Mattins and Evensong, didn't open me to that mystery. But then God touched me and awakened the idea that we are surrounded by the beauty of eternity. So when I stood by the ocean, or watched our child born or knelt in a place steeped in centuries of prayer, they carried the mystery of God. When we experience the holy we see through our fingers to the edge of God's reality.

If we have no shrine, no inner reverence, nothing that makes us catch our breath with wonder, then we close a door. I am convinced that the grotesque lack of respect for others in our society, its pornography and violence, grows where nothing is sacred.

A priest friend who has spent these days after Hillsborough in Liverpool and Sheffield said that the atmosphere at Anfield was like a Cathedral, youngsters praying and people standing in reverence. It made me think that perhaps we would not have been plunged into the years of hooliganism and violence if reverence had been the starting-point rather than the aftermath. **Thought for the Day,** 19 April 1989

The silent love of God

When I come down to my study in the morning and I sit down and think of everything that's going to happen during the day—the decisions that have to be made, the people I shall be seeing, the conflicts and demands—I can feel myself getting strung up and thinking 'it's impossible', 'I'll never get through it all'—and I wouldn't if it wasn't for the physical and emotional restoration which can come from prayer—as I discover to my cost when I miss it.

The Bible uses expressions like 'being bathed in light' or refreshed by the 'fountain of Life'. 'He makes me lie down in green meadows and leads me beside the waters of peace.' And when it describes the absence of God, it's often the same metaphor, 'The sap in me dried up as in a summer drought', 'I hunger and thirst'. Prayer is a physical and emotional experience of God—not just an activity of the brain. It is something which can soothe the tensions and tight nerves of the body, which can make us alert and more sensitive to the beauty around us—not just in the obviously beautiful, but in a person's eyes or laugh, in the way the cat's tail curls so neatly when it lies down—prayer is physical, conveys harmony. When you come to God with feelings of anger or resentment or even hate, and you pour it all out, the depression and nastiness can lose their sting. And if we get all stewed up by anxiety—'What on earth's going to happen?', 'Did I make the right choice?', 'How can I do anything about it?'—then prayer can bring calm to the storming sea.

I have always had difficulty with the teaching that says you have to go through years of dreary waiting and harrowing self-discipline and expertise before you can receive the warm beauty of the love of God. It's certainly true that prayer is sometimes empty and unrewarding, but I personally would have given up long ago if God had not always given me enough at every stage to be going on with. Of course there are tears and struggles and doubts, but there's plenty of certainty and encouragement.

Sometimes people feel cut off by the silence of God—'Why don't you say something?' 'Is there anyone there?' But that's sometimes because we misunderstand the way God gets through to us. He communicates with us in a thousand ways—a changed attitude, a new opportunity, a being forgiven, a new sympathy. He is talking to us through our physical and emotional experiences. His word to us is rarely dressed up in the supernatural—angels, a vision and thunderclouds—but rather a stream of love in natural clothing. The silence of God is not a blank concrete wall, it is for our benefit. It is rich in silent love and provides the space for God's re-creation.

Thought for the Day, 8 March 1984

A proper rhythm

We only have one life and it's important how we use it. I had a friend who learnt he had only a few months to live and every moment became precious. He spoke about the quality of time available, not the quantity.

For me two hours of second-rate television—sitcoms and American cops with happy endings—leave me exhausted, with diluted adrenalin, but if I sit by a log fire with a good book, it refreshes and heals part of me. A fire, like a river, like the sky, is alive, it's basic—of the earth, earthy—and somehow it makes me feel more put together. I could never join the fishing fraternity—I might catch a fish and have to kill it—but I can totally appreciate the cleansing and calming which flows with the stream. I find it difficult to believe that all our frenetic activity is the right way to use our time. I used to drive every day to feed a pony. I would motor to the field straight from work like a man possessed, a rat in a cage with goggles on, then I would watch the pony quietly munch away for half an hour, and be lulled back into a proper rhythm. I used to drive home from the field as though there were no deadlines, no problems, no committee meetings and all the world was gently dozing.

There is a rather melancholy book in the Bible in which the preacher says 'Emptiness, emptiness—all is empty. What does a man gain for all his labour and his toil here under the sun? Generations come and generations go, while the earth endures for ever.' Whilst we bustle around with our busyness, rush our way through life, the earth endures for ever. The writer pulls us up short as we plunge headlong into another year of harder work, a technological whirl of videos and faster life-style. At the same time the shadow over this year for millions of people will be that there is no work for them to do. It can prove a daunting question for each individual—how does he or she use the time? It puzzles me that some people are still persuaded to work even longer hours, when the harder we work the more efficient we get, the more machines we shall be able to buy to do our work for us—so it's something we shall all have to face. Somehow we've got to find a way of living which does not just depend on busyness and work for our satisfaction.

So the question I ask at the beginning of this year is, what does enrich us? What gives the best quality to our time? For me, if I get the chance, it will be having more time for my family and friends, having some moments in harmony with nature—the earth, fire, the skies—and then, what for me gives the best quality of all—stillness with God—which is the way a door quietly opens in to the infinite, where time opens up—I think I want more and more of that—to enrich the inner self, and not live so much at my nerve ends trying to sprint on the treadmill. **Thought for the Day,** 3 January 1983

Praying for rain

Last week it was reported that churches in South Africa were praying for rain because of a recent drought. It is rather different to this country, where we are usually praying for sunshine. As a vicar at a fete or a town show, people would say 'Put one in for us'. Or as the rain beats down mercilessly making the cuddly toys drip, we get the joke, 'You haven't done very well, for us, have you, vicar?'

The difficulty about all this is that one man's drought is another man's sun-tan; one country's thaw is another country's freeze-up. I often wonder how God copes with these tricky conflicts of interest. I try to imagine what it would be like for God to have to decide to send rain or not to send rain based on how much people prayed.

People talk as though God is somehow on tap to change the order of things to suit them. If a child runs out in front of a bus, it would be natural to say 'Oh God, stop the bus'. But if God does break all the rules, if He does not just use the good driving skills of the bus driver or the excellent quality of the brakes and the fact that all the drivers behind the bus are keeping their distance, if God does one of His *Acts*—an act of God—and stops the bus, overruling the normal rules of our existence . . . then He might save the child, which would be very important, but it would mean there could be no trust on our part that things normally work as they are expected to work. There could be no braking distance we could rely upon, it would be next to useless our learning to drive, the roads would become impossible because we would never know when God was going to operate the brakes.

It becomes even more difficult when God is expected to take sides. If there is a patient in the operating theatre requiring an organ, and a motor accident victim who could provide it if he died, with two sets of relatives praying, would God decide for the one or the other? Or when two countries are at war and God is expected to be on both sides—as we have seen in recent times—each side claims to be fighting a just war. Cry God for England, Harry and St George! But this is complex. There are many evils, many innocents on both sides. Disaster and suffering seem to be an almost unavoidable part of human experience. Our belief is that God grieves over both the *Belgrano* and the *Sheffield*, whatever the motives of those who created the war.

So it looks as though it's difficult to ask God to manipulate history or to change His purpose—yet it is the most profound expression where the human being hits rock bottom to cry out 'God help me!'

Christ taught three things which we hold together:

1. The rain falls on the just and the unjust. That is the natural system and it is neutral. God has not directed it in favour of some and against others. The system of the universe is set on its course, it has its own rules. The cold wind is not tempered just because the lamb has been shorn.

2. When mankind makes society or the environment go disastrously wrong by our greed and our evil, we are like the small boy who jumped on his balloon and burst it and took the ragged remains to his father and said 'Mend it!'

3. Our prayers to God should not just be said as the volcano erupts or the earth quakes or the disaster strikes; but rather prayer is a way of life, which involves us praying to God in the good times, the easy times, and prepares our whole self for the accidents, the tragic encounter we have with a brutal world set on its course.

I sympathize with those experiencing drought in South Africa, but praying for rain. . . . God may hear in His graciousness, we cannot limit Him. But the prayer must be accompanied by repentance for the system under which the country is forced to live.

The rain fell on the just and the unjust—so God ordained it.

Thought for the Day

God and the hurricane

I went to our local park yesterday and saw the devastation. Many great trees were uprooted as though some prehistoric monster had crashed through Bethnal Green. The huge roots, the gaping craters, the cars crushed, the aftermath of the hurricane. We heard the weathermen describe the deep depression which had caused it, and they traced its path and admitted its ferocity had taken them by surprise. On Thursday night I had watched out of my window and seen the huge trees in our square whipped and thrashed, bent double and broken whilst the storm continued. I felt very small and helpless before the power of nature.

For ancient people, the flood, the earthquake, the sandstorm, the lightning were all acts of God expressing His anger or carrying out His plan. As we sing in a hymn,

> His chariots of wrath the deep thunderclouds form
> And dark is His path on the wings of the storm.

But it's only insurance policies which refer to 'Acts of God'. We like to think that we have almost everything under control and there are just these irritating local disturbances which we haven't yet mastered. For a moment, we are overwhelmed and feel again the helpless, powerless feelings of mankind—so it's an Act of God. I don't think of it like that at all. I don't see floods and earthquakes and tornadoes as punishments of God, as, so to speak, deliberate acts. Rather, I think of them as part of the creation as a whole—the way the earth and the atmosphere and the universe behave. To me, the tornado is a reminder of what a continuous miracle the earth is. It spins silently through space on a course and in such a way as to allow life to flourish here. When we see the pictures of our world from a spaceship it is a beautiful sphere—as the hymn says: 'ineffably sublime'—and for most of our lives we rely on it to behave as we expect. Yet what would happen if it shifted in its course, or the sun were to cool off, or the atmosphere became dispersed or polluted? We rely day by day on a billion miracles which make our daily life possible.

The Bible teaches that the greatest danger to man is that he will think he is God—controller, governor of the earth. But it is

God who sets the planets in their courses, who made the earth firm and sure. Maybe the human race needs reminders of the normal stability of the earth which we take for granted—our hearts will pump, our brakes will work, our plants will grow, our rain will fall. And so the hurricane confronts us with our dependence upon God for the earth we inhabit. Our hymns register this fundamental difference between belief and unbelief, that there is God in and through all things. 'O tell of His might, O sing of His grace, whose robe is the light, whose canopy space.' As we look out on God's world we should always be humble and reverent—as the Bible says, the fear of the Lord is where our wisdom begins. Christ has taught us that God is love, but in that belief we should not lose the wonder at the majesty of our Creator, and the awesome power in what He has made. **Good Morning Sunday,** 18 October 1987

When disaster strikes

In the face of natural disasters, it's inevitable we should ask 'Why?' There have been times when I have found it hard to hold on to my belief in God. It's an inhuman person who sits at the bedside of a child dying, who doesn't say 'Oh, God, why?' Innocent suffering remains the most significant argument against the existence of a loving God. I gave up a long time ago thinking that we were going to prove or disprove that God exists. In the end it's a matter of whether you believe or you don't.

In the face of natural disasters I stay a believer for two main reasons. Firstly, that in the innocent suffering of *Jesus* God has shown that He can transform such events. I don't understand how *resurrection* happens, but I live in hope because Christ convinced me that it does. He demonstrated that God was in the pain and in some way bearing it and, in the end, defeating it.

Secondly, we have to come to terms with the brute realities of our world. We are set on a planet which has to abide by certain rules of nature. Man is very much at risk because of these rules, but without them life would be impossible.

The amazing stability and fertility of our earth—a multiple privilege in itself—depends upon the sun. That sun which has now become a source of peril to the people of South Australia. This is the ambiguity of nature, the blessing which can so quickly become a curse. It is the abiding reality of our earth on which we live. A minute variation in exposure to the sun and human beings are scorched. I believe that this is the unavoidable cost of the free life. The world which obeys its rules is incredibly reliable, neutral to the point of cruelty to the creatures who get caught in the wrong place at the wrong time.

Life in all its fullness cannot escape the risks of earthquake, wind and fire. When the child warming itself by the fire goes too near and burns, its parents rush to the rescue. When disaster strikes a part of the beautiful earth, the human family should do the same. **Thought for the Day,** 21 February 1983

Faith and worry

An elderly friend of mine wrote to me this week. In her letter she poured out all her worries. They are mostly the same worries which have been bugging her for years. I've never really been able to say or do anything to make them easier— only to listen and help her feel a little less alone in facing them.

Worry weighs down the world. We all know how it can drain our energy and make us feel sick and desperate. We can admit that worry does not help, but still do it. Some people are able to say to themselves 'it's no use worrying' and then get on with living. But others, however much their friends tell them not to worry, however much they say to themselves 'it's no use worrying', just can't switch off, and keep on raking over the same problem again and again.

As we go through our lives, there are times when it seems as though our worries will drown us, make us nervous and withdrawn. Worries at work, or because we haven't got work; worries at home; worries with our families and friends. Sometimes there's an impossible decision to make, and we worry till we've made it—and then worry whether it was the right decision. Anxiety about illness is very common. So many people think they have some dreadful disease, watch every possible symptom, just when their bodies need all their energy to stay well. Worry about something we've done wrong is also hard to carry—perhaps it will cause trouble? Perhaps we'll be found out?—how shameful it would be. It may be money that's the problem, perhaps we can't pay the mortgage or the heating bills. Perhaps we have responsibility for other people—our family, people who work with us, people in our care.

Whatever the cause, it can twist our tummy in knots, make us feel lousy and drag us down so that we can't tackle the problems themselves. It's something all of us experience, something we all have to tackle.

Faith, of whichever religion, offers ways through worry. Faith, in a sense, is the opposite of worry. Faith means looking our life in the face and then believing and trusting in God's care for us. We are like a child and God is like father and mother. So every morning I try to have some quiet time with God, I try to relax and say to God 'You know what a mess I am, how worried I am about all these things. Now I trust you.' It's a sort of handing over for a time to God. It needs practice, but when you grow sure that God is there it's far better than a gin, or comfort eating, or a smoke. But the night is worse than the morning— we're tired and everything looks worse and we go over and over the horrible ways things could turn out. Then I try to remember Jesus' simple, but so true, words:

> Do not be anxious about tomorrow:
> tomorrow will look after itself.
> Each day has troubles enough of its own.

Good Morning Sunday, 16 February 1986

Spiritual resources

Theology was once thought of as the Queen of Sciences. It has, for most of my life, been regarded as an archaic and inferior discipline, its insights being regarded with suspicion. A friend of mine provides an example. He has been suffering from mental

illness for twenty years, and has had every sort of treatment—
group therapy, shock treatment, analysis and, mainly, medi-
cation. In those twenty years, he came to depend upon the
drugs for anaesthetizing the terror he felt in confronting life.
Recently, he has started to come off the drugs. He has started to
discover a faith. It is, as yet, just a flicker, but it has been
enough to allay the worst of his fear and to help him hope that
he will discover within himself the resources he needs to
discover meaning and reality in his life. He told me that in all
those twenty years no therapist or doctor had ever offered him
any idea that he might find a clue in faith, or that spiritual
resources were a possible source of strength. In fact, at those
times when he had raised the question, this search for faith was
regarded by the professionals as a 'cop-out', a running away
from the tension of the reality which he was thought to be too
terrified to face. It was as though they were saying to the
hungry man, 'You are not hungry, there is no bread'. Of course,
religion can be a most neurotic response to life, but it is not
necessarily so. All those who deny its possibility will have to
accept responsibility—if God turns out to be true—that they cut
off many a needy human being from the resources of faith, its
knowledge, its healing, its strength, its forgiveness, which none
of their technology and medicine were able to replace.

Now I detect a growing and welcome humility amongst the
'experts'. There seems to be a new recognition that we have to
take the whole person into account, not just our environment,
not just our body, not just our personality, but also our purpose
and meaning, the mystery of our motives. **Half Way**

Freud and faith

What Freud and others have failed to see is that the God many
of us have discovered is like the loving father and mother who
want nothing more for their children than that they should
become mature, loving human beings, pouring their love and
faith and hope into the common weal. It is a mistake we often
make that when we criticize other people's belief and ideology,
we compare our own best understanding of our own belief

with the worst examples of theirs! Christians have excelled at this sleight of hand in treating other religions and ideologies. But it is as foolish, because religion is often perverted, for the non-believers to close their eyes to its great truth, as it is absurd for Christians to ignore the essential secular insights which have transformed our understanding of the human personality and the universe. As R. S. Lee gently remarked,

> Atheism will . . . tend to betray its infantile origin by its preoccupation in a negative way with the idea of God.
>
> *Freud and Christianity*, p. 125

It is just as possible for a person to eliminate God through illusion and wish-fulfilment and fear as it is to create him. A map which excludes the reality of God is like a chart which omits to mark the sea. To my view, so many of the needs and hunger and trauma described in the case-studies from which the maps are drawn, are signs of the omission of God from the scene. I am not producing God out of a hat to solve life's problems like a magician, rather like those who say 'Harrow your hearers until they are well and truly frightened and depressed and then bring out your Christ'. Nor am I trying to calculate some sort of equation in which, by amazing coincidence, X = Christ, but rather to talk about the Christian vision of man in its attempt to unravel 'the person within'. I believe it is an interpretation which still has a great deal to offer believer and non-believer alike, and provides a map worthy of study.

Half Way

The cell in my mind

A sermon preached in Pentonville prison, Christmas Day 1989

People partly make us what we are—mothers, fathers, friends, enemies. But we are also made in a place where it's just us—'a secret room' where I am me. In that room in my mind—am I alone? However much we share our thoughts with others, we also know well that place where it is just us in conversation with ourselves. Here in prison you know that place better than most. There, they seem to be our thoughts, the answers seem to be our answers. We seem to know ourselves so well, we know just how to talk to ourselves, we speak the same language. Our skull is not only a protection for the brain, but in a way the hard walls of the cell in which we all live. It is there in that cell that we all begin, it is there that Christmas is shut down or opened up. The question we face in our mind is, 'is there God?' Do these conversations in our minds, our feelings, our thinking, contain God speaking to us? When we cry out, is the cry heard, when we feel thankful, is there God to thank, when we are almost mad with rage, is there God to bear the brunt of our anger?

In the Bible it says, 'The fool has said in his heart there is no God'. Certainly, the great majority of people till now have believed there is a God. But without a 'yes' to the question of God, Christmas is a fairy story, a good excuse for a booze up at a party, little else. God is the key question, and on the answer depends the whole conduct of our lives. If there is God there is meaning to my life, there is a demand on my life—I live it for someone other than myself—there is a wonderful comfort in my life—I am never alone, never abandoned to my fate. If He is a loving God then my life is transformed because at its heart there is what I most inwardly desire—namely, the love of another.

But once we admit the possibility of God, there follows the further question—just as important and just as much on the minds of people of all ages—'What is God like?' Perhaps God is evil? There's plenty of evidence, in ourselves, in the world around us, of pain and wickedness—but we'd have to ask why there is so much good, why there is beauty and truth and love and hope, why children are born, why we fall in love, why the height of the mountains, why the stars, why a mother's love, why the laughter of friends, why companionship, why goodness, if God invisible is evil?

In spite of all our own shame, there is also a hope about us. The witness of the Bible is that God is, God communicates, God listens, God is always trying to get through to us, He stands at the door and knocks. The signals sometimes are in code, sometimes there is serious interference, but nevertheless God is real and reaches out to us. The meaning of Christmas is simply this—that the God of all peoples, of all creation, without whom nothing was made, through whom we, from our first life in the womb until now, have our lives—that God exists. But, and this is why the Christian is happy and full of inward peace, if that God has been given a human face in Christ it is as though a great laser beam, a spotlight, has penetrated into the skies and lit up God for us to see, so in one sense we know who we are talking to, whom we are trusting, who is with us, who heals our wounds, who forgives our sins.

So Christ is in us all, whether we turn towards him or away from him. I find every day I do both. A close friend of mine had a heart transplant and two near-death experiences. In one he saw a wonderful light and knew he was with Christ—when he came round he wanted to go back. The other was frightening— he saw the light but there was a figure crouching in the corner, the light was all around him but he didn't see it, he was shrouded in himself.

That's like my life, when I follow Christ—love him and do his will—I feel the encouragement, the happiness, the sense of the rightness of life. When I turn my back on him, as I do, I feel shame and self-dislike. In a funny way this is an encourage- ment, it teaches me that my happiness, my fulfilment lie in the love of God—following Christ.

The point about God which is so strong today, Christmas Day, is that He never turns his back, never says 'no' to anyone who turns to Him, you don't have to go anywhere to be open to Him, it costs nothing except the desire. He is always waiting, whatever darkness we are and have been involved in, however many masks we wear to the outside world, if in that inmost self, the person who is me, is you, right in our hearts where we see, talk with ourselves, there we admit we want God, love God, yearn for the peace that God gives. If we stay still, if we pray, even if we just say 'Oh God help me', 'Oh God forgive me', these are real prayers and they work.

So Christmas stands for the greatest gift of life, the gift of God to each of us. The other day I confirmed three prisoners at Holloway, two of them had committed serious crimes, the Chaplain said we started with six, but three have been ac- quitted. I said that the point of Christ is that we are all acquitted, when we recognize what we have done and are truly sorry. We are all acquitted before God, we are forgiven, we are free in ourselves, and this is the beginning of the road to freedom itself.

So I pray that as you have to spend Christmas Day here, you will pray, you will talk simply to God, entrust yourselves to

Him, because He is like Christ, and the peace of Christ is for you all.

May God bless you and those whom you love, protect you and them this Christmas Day. Amen.

Not good enough for church

It is my belief that hope is a beautiful gift of God, and it can be found and unwrapped in prayer. It is sad, however, to see the number of people who say they are too miserable, too unhappy, to pray. Sometimes people will stay away from church for months, and then say that they have felt too miserable to come. It is almost as though they are determined not to let God off the hook either. People say, 'I'm not good enough to go to church'. When you think of the nature of Jesus, his teaching and his promise, you can appreciate why the opposite should be true—'I'm not good enough *not* to go'. But prayer doesn't just happen in church, and it is important to remember that it is the God of hope as well as of love to whom we pray. There seems to be an internal personal mystery which takes a person out of self-pity and self-hurt into hope and a rebuilding of the sense of identity. **Half Way**

The human scale

There haven't been many television programmes which have aroused as much comment as Prince Charles's fine documentary on architecture. Yet in all the talk, a keystone of his analysis has been largely ignored. Commentators have concentrated on 'the human scale'—on dehumanizing, alien buildings, but have said little about the way that scale is measured—that is, through the perspective of our relationship with God.

Remember those psychological tests given to children when they were asked to draw a picture of their house and a tree?

The scale they gave to each gave a clue to the way the children saw their lives. If we were to take a photograph of a person standing at the foot of a mountain and include the whole mountain in the picture, the person would become a speck. When we stand at the edge of the ocean we are touched with awe at our smallness. When an astronaut looks out of his spaceship is he a wide-eyed child exploring God's universe, or is he master of all he surveys?

For those who believe in God, the human scale can only be truly known when compared with the divine. It is the soaring majesty of God which puts us in perspective. To leave God out of the scheme of things is to distort our own part in it all. I felt that Prince Charles was reminding a very secular society that although the map of the universe doesn't show God anywhere, we still owe our existence to Him.

The Bible contains some sharp cartoons along this line. Isaiah says 'To God, the nations are just like drops in a bucket, the coasts and islands weigh like specks of dust'. And the Psalmist asks God, 'When I look at thy Heavens and the work of thy fingers . . . what is man that thou shouldst remember him?' But, nevertheless, though we are small, to God we have great significance—as the Psalm goes on to say, 'Yet you have made him little less than a God'.

As Prince Charles demolished a concrete stack of garages which have been an eyesore in Bow for years, I felt like cheering. I was reminded of that Tower built in Babel which lay in ruins in the desert like a pyramid to warn passers-by what happens when human beings claim to be like God.

In our generation we face so many life and death issues which turn on our capacity for humility before God, and our reverence for His world—the way we farm His land, the way we breed His creatures, the way we exploit His mineral resources, our inhumanity to His children. We don't like to recognize our dependence on God, it seems to reduce us, but the reverse is true, it gives us our human scale.

Thought for the Day, 22 November 1988

What is God giving us?

Our prayer in part is to remind ourselves that we are receiving the love of God, not forcing it by our own efforts, not creating it by our anxiety, and not earning it by our goodness. Whether we need to be humbled or encouraged, a key is to discover what life God is giving us. Being open to His love has this wonderful way of exalting the humble and bringing down the arrogant in each of us. The promotion is not everything, the success is not all-important. However anxious we get we cannot grow half an inch. We cannot drive ourselves to be happy, we cannot drive ourselves to be born, we cannot make ourselves perfect. We cannot live two lives in one, we cannot insure ourselves against suffering—in all these things we depend upon the inbreathing of God.

> Then the Lord God formed man from the dust of the ground and breathed into his nostrils the breath of life.
>
> *Genesis* 2.7

This dependence is the fundamental attitude and starting place of the good life. So, if we are successful people, let's see it for what it is—see through it and retain a reverence for others. If we are a failure, trust in God, recognize through faith that He has a destiny for us. Dignity is within, conferred by the love of God. **Half Way**

Good laughter

A friend said to me that she picked up an undercurrent of sadness in my 'Thoughts for the Day'. Although there *is* a lot to be sad about in the inner cities, *gloom* would not fairly represent the atmosphere, because people laugh a lot, often in the face of great difficulties. *Laughter* seems to be a crucial part of the survival kit.

I once did a little amateur research of the subject in the Bible, to see what *it* had to say about one of God's best medicines. I expected to find a wealth of material, because my strongest image of Jewish family life was one of laughter in the face of great adversities, and my Christian experience has proved that faith in Christ brings a full happiness. But, strangely, almost every example I found was not *good* laughter but bad. That distinction was interesting in itself.

There was the word which meant '*Laughing scorn*'—mocking unfortunate people—such as when children jeer at a fat boy, or when the clever taunt the simple. Then there was the *cynical* laughter, enshrined in the Bible in the name Isaac, which means laughter; because when God told Abraham that his wife Sarah, who was long past the age of child-bearing, was going to have a son, Abraham fell about laughing, and so did Sarah who was listening behind the tent door—and they called the baby Isaac! Then there's *hollow* laughter which covers up an inner despair, like the broadcaster who tries to liven up an interview with an incredibly dull speaker, or the canned laughter injected into a feeble script. Then there is also *escapist* laughter, covering for fear—let us eat, drink, and be merry, for tomorrow we die!— or at least have a hangover.

These examples are hardly calculated to lift the Monday morning blues. They give us a useful negative idea—namely that not all laughter is good—but what's the positive? You'll find it in the Bible if you look up a different word, one we rarely use because it's become rather pious—the word is *joy*. Yet I think we vicars should go on risking the mirth of the rest of the world, because there's an important point made in the distinction between laughter and joy.

Compare, in a family, the teasing which *everyone enjoys* because it expresses the affection and trust which exists, with the mockery of a parent or brother or sister which slips over into the scorn which hurts and destroys confidence. Sarah's cynical no-hope laughter turned to joy when her child was born. The hollow laughter of a dirty joke in a lonely London pub is empty compared with the fun of two people enjoying the harmony of an old friendship. It's also true that laughter sometimes seems at its best when people are up against it together. Perhaps there will be a laugh or two at the village tap today during the freeze-up.

Good laughter is the happiest expression of human affection. But the Bible would have us believe that as *joy* is divine in origin, like the baby's chuckle which rewards our clowning, it

32

comes direct and unstained from God, and is the smile on the human face which believes that God loves us.

Thought for the Day, 24 January 1983

A notion of the Devil

We live in a world where evil is still unchecked, in spite of all our new technology and knowledge. The picture of life as a conflict between good and evil is important for us as individuals and as a race. The mythology which Jesus accepted was as much a part of his way of looking at life and God, as our myths are part of us. In a time of cheap and transient myths, it may be important for us to have a new humility towards the world view of the Son of Man.

We do not have to travel far to explore the reality of evil, because it can and should be studied in the battlefield of our own mind. If we find it there, we can be sure that in the affairs of society, in the great affairs of the nations, it will be rampant. I am convinced that some of the bad things I have done and imagined are not just the result of being hard-done-by. The hurts which I have received have seemed to make me more ready to hurt others, but it is difficult to escape the idea that some of my worst thoughts and actions arrive in my mind under their own power. The conversation in my mind suggests that there is a voice or an impulse which offers me the bad alternative. I can then have all sorts of arguments with another voice or set of impulses which try to prevent me. Is this just the 'computerized' response based on my past experience? Am I programmed to respond in this way by the 'parent' in me, or by the hurt I have suffered in the past? It is puzzling, if that is the case, that I can analyse and explain it to myself, point out all the possible damage it will do, yet at the same time do it. The sources of evil in myself could be in part the result of stored resentment and anger, and in part the replay of the strongest and most passionate experiences on my own tape, in part the fearful reaction to the threatened loss of love. Yet those descriptions do not seem to me to describe adequately the independence of the evil within me. I am led to believe that the

33

impulse, the energy and the will behind the evil I have done are not just a facet of my past experience, but rather a reality against which I have to struggle.

It is amazing how the energy and ammunition of evil is primed and ready to spring into action. It is so hard for the good in me to thrive. It is as though there is a computer operator deliberately selecting the difficult memories or playing the most depressing tapes. We do have considerable control over which tapes we play. We can, to some extent, choose to listen or to reject them. We are sometimes hooked on the damaging and difficult ones. But that does not seem a sufficient explanation, and I am left with the question, 'Is this computer operator the hidden function of my own self, or is there some transcendent source?' Those of us who believe in God, believe that God can be positively involved in our thinking and feeling. We also believe that the Spirit of God can enter our consciousness. It is not difficult to believe that there is an accuser, a tempter, a stimulus of the evil. André Gide quotes *The Deliverance of Mark Rutherford*, volume 2, p. 113:

> The shallowest of mortals is able now to laugh at the notion of a personal devil. No doubt there is no such thing existent; but the horror at evil which could find no other expression than in the creation of a devil is no subject for laughter, and if it does not in some shape or other survive, the race itself will not survive. No religion, so far as I know, has dwelt like Christianity with such profound earnestness on the bisection of man—on the distinction within him, vital to the very last degree, between the higher and the lower, heaven and hell. What utter folly is it because of an antique vesture to condemn as effete what the vesture clothes! Its doctrine and its sacred story are fixtures in concrete form of precious thoughts purchased by blood and tears.
>
> *Journals 1889–1949*, p. 241

Jesus believed there was the evil one—the evil side—the prince of darkness. It emerged through the mind and heart of man, both individually and corporately, and it had to be fought. The mythology was a way of describing this evil. Nothing could be more dangerous than to underestimate the reality of evil—except possibly to credit it with too much power. Whether this tendency to do wrong comes from within myself or within the human race, its reality is vivid and challenges us to fight the good fight. We have the drama of the struggle. If the darkness and shadow are not part of the portrait, the human being is drawn in pale pastel and bears little resemblance to the sharply defined conflict of our experience. The battle within us is not just an unravelling of the self and the maturity of the 'adult' who is there in waiting, because when the adult emerges he will still have the battle against evil. The more maturity, the deeper the perceptions, the higher the virtue—the stronger will be the sensitivity to evil and the ensuing battle. **Half Way**

Bursting a blood vessel

We first moved into London seventeen years ago. At that time, whenever I heard a row in the street, I used to dash outside, as an eager young curate, in case someone was getting hurt. But through the years I have heard so much anger it's almost become background noise. Sometimes it's anger over the most trivial things, like being made to wait a long time outside a phone box, a referee's mistake, or a self-assembly kit that doesn't and won't. It's very close to the surface, this anger, pent up and so easily sparked. It is at the root of much of the gratuitous violence in the city.

I am interested in anger—and because I get angry and am ashamed when I do, I hope to understand it. Why do I lose my temper (there's an interesting expression, because it *is* a loss)? When I think about it afterwards, I know I have dented my own self-respect. How much better it would have been if I had dealt with it quietly and firmly and not lost control. But it's odd, too, that sometimes I have felt ashamed of getting angry and other people present have been grateful. So perhaps it's not all bad. That is certainly confirmed by the Bible, where anger is both bad and good.

We first learn how to get angry in childhood. When a two-year-old lies on the floor of the supermarket screaming because he can't have a lolly, everyone smiles, except his poor parents. Rage in an infant may be tolerable, but the same rage in adult form is unpleasant and dangerous. Someone described this sort of anger as 'the mobilization of extreme effort to gain what we want by our own exertion'. Bursting blood vessels, blowing our tops, tearing our hair out, all suggest the intense physical exertion involved in anger. There is a Hebrew word which means both anger and heat. Of course, the more clever we are with words, and the more we have power over other people, the less we need to use personal physical violence to get our own way. We can see the contrast every day in the newspapers and on television—lethal sophisticated phrases may release the anger for the articulate and gain what they want, whereas someone who has fewer words and is powerless will more quickly resort to his fists and his boot. But this anger—to get what we want—whether clever or inarticulate, is an extreme form of selfishness—mobilization of extreme effort—the use of all our power and resources to get our own way. However we may deceive ourselves or disguise it as righteous anger, it is at heart an extreme form of self-assertion.

Jesus, as usual, will have none of our excuses. 'Anyone who nurses anger against his brother must be brought to judgement.' This 'getting our own way' anger is one of the things which needs to be exposed to the love of God because in experiencing that love we learn that 'getting our own way' rarely makes us happy, and the satisfaction gained from getting our own way by the use of anger soon passes, and changes to shame.

Thought for the Day, 20 September 1983

Anger–a technique for self-preservation

Anger as a technique of self-preservation is learnt in child-hood—by the screaming infant who wants more milk, or the small child's bawling battle for survival against brothers and sisters. Then there's our adolescent anger to establish identity over against parents and defend loyalties to friends. By the time we are adults, our anger is ready to erupt whenever we are seriously threatened as an individual or as a family. Anyone who attacks them, attacks me.

For some people, this anger is learnt far too well—children who have never known the security of home, have had their trust betrayed over and over again or have been damaged by the education system and their environment, often develop anger, almost as a way of life, as a desperate attempt to hold on to their identity.

It's also true that in our big cities the hectic aggression of the life around us produces stress, and it can make life feel like a fight for survival. There seems to be much less anger in rural communities. Forty-eight homes in a solid block will nearly always produce more anger than homes spread through a country village with space to unwind and somewhere nearby where we can escape from the pressure and from people. It's one of the human miracles that there's still so much fun and good humour in our cities.

So what do we do with this self-righteous anger? In part, it's a necessity. It may be the only way to defend ourselves. And if we try to suppress it, it often squeezes out as sly nastiness or explodes with even greater force. We don't find it easy to cope with, yet at the same time, when we, or those whom we love, are threatened or hurt we need to express it. The child or adult who gets totally beaten down by other people may end up as a doormat or disturbed. Or when someone we love dies in a cruel way, it's important that any anger against God or life has to be released before healing can begin.

But how much of our anger is about essential self-preservation? Often it's just self-indulgence—because someone has criticized us, or because a remark hits the target of our guilt. On reflection, much that seems to threaten us is not very significant, and we feel better in the morning. So how far should our self-preservation anger be allowed to go?

The picture we have of Jesus is significant. When his life was threatened he did not retaliate—quietly taking the injustice—but then he didn't have a wife and children to defend and, perhaps more important, his own identity and security in God were so great that, as he said, even the people putting him to death could not threaten him.

It's only when our identity is secure and our faith in God is strong that the commandment to love our enemies and to pray for those who spitefully use us seems even remotely possible, because our self becomes more secure and less in need of anger to defend it. We can begin to practise it in small ways and perhaps, bit by bit, begin to quieten the city's volcano.

Thought for the Day, 21 September 1983

Righteous anger

At first sight, 'righteous anger' seems to be more acceptable, stemming from a concern not for ourselves, but for others. But even here we need to remember our infinite capacity for self-deception. 'The heart is deceitful above all things', as Jeremiah put it. We may unleash our rage in the belief that we care, or that we have right on our side, yet our motives would not bear close examination.

For example—on the domestic level, a husband or wife whose marriage is breaking up may appear to have the children's best interests at heart, but in fact is using them to score points. Or, in the community, we sometimes suffer the angry rhetoric of people who take up a cause not because they truly care for those who are suffering, not because they have listened to them and got inside their struggle, but because their righteous anger may gain them political advantage and personal power. Or again, at the international level, the leaders of a nation fulminate against other nations about some infringement of human liberty when they themselves order and support exactly the same practices.

We often take out our own unhappiness and resentment in anger against this or that—use someone else's suffering as a means of letting off steam about our own grievances. The passionate desire to punish, so much a feature of our society, is often based not upon righteousness, but the search for a scapegoat for our own inner problems.

This is not to say that there is no such thing as righteous anger. Jesus certainly got angry. On behalf of God—when he drove out the profiteers from the temple; on behalf of the poor—in his fearful warnings to the rich, against religious hypocrites who were all very holy in public but inside were rotten, or against the force of evil which tried to tempt and ensnare him.

Jesus also reflected the anger of God. It's strange that in such an angry century as ours we have quietly discounted the anger of God. As though we believed He watched the little children shuffle into Auschwitz with unruffled calm, or now watches so many of His children starve when there is so much wealth and food in the world. For most of us, the threat of hell is no longer a reality, and the wrath of God only appears on cranky sandwich-boards. But in the desire to soften the damaging dread of God and emphasize His love, it's been too easy to water our view of Him—as though anything we do will pass before the smile of His kind and undemanding judgement.

I believe there is anger in God's love. Even if the way that anger is portrayed sometimes says more about us than it does about Him. I also believe that those who work and share the suffering of the poor and maltreated—who sit where they sit—will be a channel of that righteous concern of God—the anger which is rooted in compassion.

Thought for the Day, 22 September 1983

'Leave your ego at the door'

As long as I can remember, I have liked winning—whether it was scheming to beat my sister at Monopoly or watching West Ham and pouring mostly silent abuse on the referee. 'Competing' seems to express some essential part of our personality. It looks as though it's a key to what's called the human *race*. We appear to be fascinated by competition—not only against others, but we try to break every imaginable record. There are Oscars, Superstars, Masterminds, EMIs, Young Business persons of the year. From the most basic rivalry between two stags for a harem of hinds, to the highly sophisticated struggle between multi-national companies to discover the technology which will give them the lead—competition rules! We believe we *have* to compete to survive the economic and material perils of living in our world—and behind our fragile earth's partial peace lies the most deadly competition of all—the arms race.

Competition stretches our human ability—if only I could be Daley Thompson and not just Jim Thompson—it increases our muscle power, our inventiveness and our excellence. But there is a turning point when it becomes a negative force. We speak of cut-throat competition, the law of the jungle, the point when the loyalty of football fans becomes gang warfare, or when a businessman cuts safety corners to cut costs, or when one nation robs another of its resources. Because for every winner there is a loser—sometimes a million losers. There is a wall round an Ethiopian hunger camp—those inside the wall will survive, those outside the wall will starve to death. They have failed to win the smallest crumb which falls from the rich man's table.

So there are limits to competition. We would not boast about defeating a handicapped child, or getting rich by outwitting the blind. For the Christian there is a big question here, because Jesus was a loser by almost every definition of worldly winning. He had no home, no wife, no family, no security, few possessions, no power. He preached a gospel of co-operation, of brotherhood, of caring for the weak. His teaching puts a severe check upon unbridled competition. I wonder how God views our human race which spends so much on arms and such vast sums on maintaining only one-third of its members.

I like to remember Band Aid—all those stars who usually compete to be top of the pops. As they went into the recording studio to make their record for Ethiopia, they saw a notice which read 'Leave your ego at the door'. Jesus said something rather similar—leave self behind and follow me.

Thought for the Day, 14 May 1985

Victorious victim

Jesus was an uncompetitive man—very far from the advertisers' macho super male. He left his ego at the door, and became an innocent victim of injustice. I suppose that's one of the reasons why so many suffering people have loved him—because he was one of them. He identified with the losers and victims of his own society, not just with pious words, but in life-style and action. He was sometimes overwhelmed by the poor, the lepers, the blind, the mentally sick—and finally shared the death of a criminal. To me, his words to the thief on the cross are beautiful. 'Truly this day you will be with me in paradise.'

But if Jesus had just been a loser and a victim, I wonder if people would have staked their lives on him for 2,000 years? Most innocent victims are a cause for despair, not hope. After Jesus died, strange things happened. People didn't completely understand what was going on. His friends were confused, but they were all convinced that in some way the death barrier had been broken. That's as much of a mystery for us as it was for them. But however uncertain they might have been about what exactly happened, they were sure—absolutely 100 per cent—that Jesus, loser and victim, was the eventual winner. Not in the sense of the world's winning, but that even the greatest evils would be overcome and the sorrows of mankind healed. This victory depended upon the reality of paradise—God's place, God's dimension, where Jesus and the thief would be together. This paradise was not to be a divine excuse for doing nothing about hell on earth—'Don't worry my child, your belly is swollen with hunger, but you'll be fine in paradise'—rather it made people even more determined to struggle till the world could be more like paradise. People who had a proper vision of justice and peace in heaven passionately wanted it here on earth as well.

Today Christians celebrate the feast of the Ascension. To many people that must seem a pretty way-out word. But for us, it's basically the reason why we keep cheerful—well, fairly cheerful—in what can seem a pretty drizzly world. Because we believe that in spite of all the frustrations and miseries it's well worth going on trying to make it a better place—and that losers and victims somehow share in the death-defying victory of Christ, both here and in paradise.

Thought for the Day, 16 May 1985

Not redundant to God

Last week I spent some time with a friend who is being made redundant. We had to go through the complicated documents and study the terms he was being offered. There were two main issues he was facing—first, how it was going to affect his income—the money. Secondly, how he was going to spend his time.

How does a hard-working person who has given most of his life to work suddenly face redundancy and a reduced income? The money is important. We all know that, and a lot of talk and thought goes into that—but the second question, 'How am I going to spend my time?', is also important when we think about our happiness.

The word 'redundant' itself can be extremely depressing. It can be a cruel word. This was brought home by a newspaper article about me last week. The headline asked, 'Is the Bishop redundant?'

Strictly speaking, 'redundant' means surplus to requirements—no longer needed. Work is one large area in our life where we are needed—where we have to turn up. Where we have to do the job—where people depend upon us. If that's wiped away it can leave a great big void—and it's only too easy to begin thinking 'I'm useless' and feeling rejected.

Although some see it as a new start—a new chance to do the things they've always wanted to do—others experience it as a shock—as though the ground was pulled away from under them—they think they are on the scrap-heap.

When the newspaper article asked if I was redundant, I thought for a moment—What do I do?—I don't make anything useful—I'm certainly not contributing to the nation's wealth. I am not helping the export drive—in fact according to some definitions I haven't done a proper day's work in my life since I stopped being an accountant. Yet I am fully employed! I spend most of my time with people. When I look at any use I might be, it would have to be measured in terms of—'I encouraged Charlie and he survived'—'I took the sting out of an angry row between two people'—'I supported some community enterprise'—'I perhaps helped some young person back on the straight and narrow'. I don't know whether I've achieved these sort of things—that's not the point—the point is that human need is all around us. There is so much that needs to be done—both with people and practical tasks. In the community no one should be redundant. We are all needed—needed to do things most of us can do.

For those of us who believe in God it is even clearer—we are needed by God—because we are His hands, His feet, His eyes, His voice—we are His agents and He has branches everywhere.

Good Morning Sunday, 9 March 1985

Premature miracle

Late one evening, I was taken by one of our deacons to visit the premature baby unit in her local hospital. I wonder if you've ever been to such a place. It's a land of many miracles. In earlier times most of the babies would have died at birth, but there they are in their little greenhouses—rather like space modules—with their delicate tiny bodies wired and taped to record their heartbeat, feeding them, bathing them in artificial sunlight. Amazing little humans at the centre of those complicated machines and recorders which are trying to replace the secure environment provided normally by their mother in the womb.

Every now and then a buzzer would go and a nurse would go across to one of the babies, put a hand in through a Perspex window, give the baby a gentle prod and say cheerfully, 'Stop slacking, George', 'Come on Mary, breathe'. On the wall are photos of the progress made by babies who arrived with only a slim chance of survival, and have left for home in the arms of thankful parents.

It's rather like a sneak preview of what normally happens in the womb. Almost as though we were having a private show of what God does naturally in secret. When you think, those little people would normally be fed, monitored, linked in with their mother's system, growing from a minute beginning, providing fingers and toes and eyes and ears and brains—complicated nervous system, intricate muscles and bones. If they are born premature we have to provide the most incredibly sophisticated machinery, intensive care, security against infection. It seems impossible that all this would be the result of some accident, a random chance of evolution. There was one little baby who was severely handicapped, but the abnormal makes you realize the wonderful miracle of the normal, and I felt a deep sense of worship.

There is a beautiful psalm which exactly captures this sense of the majesty of God:

For you have created my inward parts
you knit me together in my mother's womb
Your eyes saw my limbs when they were yet imperfect

and in your book were all my members written
day by day were they fashioned.

To see this miracle and all the technology of nature it depends on, to see the heart pumping beneath the silky skin, to see the fingers perfect and curled on the white sheet, was for me to experience God. No wonder the psalmist said:

I will praise you—wonderful are your works.

So as we look and see, as we see the nurses and doctors sharing in these miracles, we are reminded that we too made that journey from seed, to womb, to life. And perhaps we should stop for a moment in the middle of our busy, self-filled lives and remember that love of God which created us, and now surrounds us with His blessing.

Good Morning Sunday, 28 June 1987

Blind fear

I wonder if you saw on the news the pictures of the small boy who fell into the gorilla pit. He was leaning over the parapet in a zoo in Jersey, trying to get a better view, when he fell out of his dad's hands, and crashed to the ground. Everyone shouted at him to keep still, for fear that he would disturb the gorillas and invite them to attack him. The biggest gorilla of all was just near where he fell. The massive animal reached forward and delicately and gently touched the boy, as if he was giving comfort. After a short while, the lad came to, saw the gorilla and naturally screamed. This scream frightened the gorilla and it ran off.

I've been thinking about this amazing event. We all seem to have assumed that the gorilla would attack the boy. Perhaps if we knew gorillas well we would not have been surprised, but rather have expected that it would protect the child in this way. Gorillas, like us, have strong protective feelings towards a small wounded member of their own family. Of course there may be good evidence that humans have a real cause to be frightened of gorillas, but I would guess that gorillas have much more cause to be terrified of humans.

We often are frightened of animals or insects when there's no real cause—it's just what we imagine. We're like that with other people too—in our minds we are terrified or angry or hating before we've even had a chance to get to know the person in question. Fear is infectious. A horse will sense a rider's fear and often then behave in a mad way, which made the rider afraid in the first place. Fear produces a vicious circle of violence. It's often based on total ignorance of what is alien to us.

I remember as a boy being afraid of one of my schoolteachers. I could hardly believe it was the same person when I met him ten years later. It's especially true of our fear of foreigners—we don't understand their language, their customs, and we are often afraid of what seems alien to us. But so often in my life I've found that when I've sat in the person's kitchen, or shared their tent, or a car journey, and got to know them, I can't think what I was afraid of. Our fear exaggerates the power of the person we're afraid of, we're blinded by it.

There's a clever advert on the television which shows three different pictures of the same event. The first shows a tough skinhead charging up a street, the second shows him apparently attacking an old man to steal his briefcase, the third shows the whole picture—the skinhead is trying to save the man from falling masonry.

Our fear often distorts what we see—especially in the way we look at people who don't fit easily into what we are used to or what we know. **Good Morning Sunday,** 7 September 1986

Angels, Archangels

One of our local churches in Bow is putting on a Nativity play. Most of the parts will be played by grown-ups, and the other night I met the shepherds' angel. There and then she proclaimed her part in no uncertain terms: 'Don't be afraid', she said, 'I have some good news for you, there is great joy coming to all the people. Today in the city of David a Saviour has been born!'

Our angel was a local granny and she was word-perfect. There was no doubting *her* existence. Yet I wondered about the angel who had appeared to the shepherds. And what about the angels who appear in the Easter story? Do I believe in them? Do you believe in them? Angels are literally messengers of God. Sometimes they are ordinary people who say something to you or do something for you, and you feel that somehow God sent them as angels of mercy. That happened to me several times. I remember being in a crash in Africa many miles from any-where—I had broken my arm—the Landrover was severely damaged. We hadn't seen a car or a person all day. A car approached and out stepped a smart man who said he was the Anglican representative of the Church of Zambia. He was a sort of angel.

But what about the lights in the sky and the shining robes—that's more difficult. There are many people who think they are just poetic licence—but I'm not so sure. Just because I've never seen a glorious angel doesn't mean they might not have appeared when Christ was born or when he rose from the dead. It's flimsy evidence to say they *couldn't* happen because *we* have never seen them.

When we look around our doomwatch world it's difficult to believe in angels, yet the world of Joseph and Mary was also frightening and disheartening. They were refugees but the glory of God came into their lives through the eyes of the wise men and the shepherds so they were able to see the beauty of heaven through the little incomparable miracle of the birth of their baby. Suddenly their frightening, depressing world had meaning and hope again. I wonder if we are all so blind to the eternal dimension around us that we need heavenly beings to break through our so down-to-earth view of things. Perhaps if there had been no angels we would have had our eyes down and never noticed the birth of Christ.

In the worship of the Church there is a great saying, 'with angels and archangels and all the company of heaven'. Perhaps the company of heaven couldn't resist having their say when they saw the great love of God in sending a Saviour to us. Perhaps now in the twentieth century it's the only way they can make us look up from all our busyness to look towards the wonder of God. If we have open minds, angels can still be effective messengers and persuade us that a Saviour was born in the city of David. **Good Morning Sunday,** 14 December 1986

Life as vocation

I know how irritating and unjust it can be when people say 'teaching is a vocation' and make it a reason for paying teachers less. The same argument has been used with clergy and nurses. But, in the proper battle for recognition, teachers should not surrender the best vision to materialism, because their job *is* vocation.

It's always a risk to indulge in derivation on *Thought for the Day*, under the ear of the experts—last time I got it wrong—but the Latin word *vocare* means 'to call', and a person with a vocation is called to respond to someone or something beyond themselves. For religious people it is a calling from God.

This weekend when our Bishop ordained priests and deacons in St Paul's he challenged them—'Do you believe, so far as you know your own heart, that God has called you?' This reflects the many callings in the Bible, to Samuel as a boy sleeping by the altar of the Lord, to Moses called to lead his people out of slavery in Egypt, and the simple words of Jesus to his disciples, 'Come follow me'.

Christians, like people of many faiths, believe that all our lives are a vocation towards God. This is so different to much of the propaganda, which suggests that the key factor in a job is how much it pays because it can buy what we want.

I was encouraged the other day by a young man who told me he was giving up his job in computers to be a dancer, not because computers aren't important, but because he was responding to his muse. To have a vocation, to be responding to God, or to social need, or to a creative talent is to give life a sense of purpose. **Thought for the Day,** 4 July 1989

The sense of purpose

I remember so well the hard time I had when leaving school. People kept asking me 'What are you going to do?' I hadn't a clue, and I drifted into training as a chartered accountant. It would be difficult to imagine a job less suited to me. I fast discovered that battles with the Inland Revenue would never satisfy my inner man.

I remember the excitement I felt when I discovered the sense of purpose I was searching for—the love of God and the brotherhood of man. Whatever happened to the brotherhood of man? Perhaps it was just one of those naive ideals so popular in the sixties. I got hooked on it because Christ lived it and taught it. To me, it was a moment of revelation when we prayed about the service of God being perfect freedom. This ideal freed me from the narrow gauge of the self, and I set out to be a priest. I did not feel that by doing so I was down-grading my life, because its value had nothing to do with the size of the salary. We used words like 'vocation', believing we were called to serve God and our fellow human beings.

I realize now that accountants also are important, that society needs to create wealth and people who are enthusiastic about it, because we need resources not only for our own nation but for the whole brotherhood of man. But I regret the apparent devaluing of lives which are not dominated by commercial goals, because money seems to have become the main measure of what's worthwhile. I am also sure that if people approach a life in commerce without some spiritual framework, or sense of purpose beyond themselves, they will be pursued by Jesus' haunting words about gaining the whole world and forfeiting the true self. **Thought for the Day,** 11 May 1988

Access!

———

Last week I had the new experience of opening an account in a shop. I sat down in a sort of cubicle and a friendly lady behind the counter asked for my name and address. Then she said, 'Have you got any proof of your identity?' I produced a credit card and she had to check it on the computer. Then she asked for my driving licence, and after one glance, she said gently but with a touch of steel, 'That's a different address!' There on the licence was our old address of four years ago. By this time, I was almost doubting whether I was genuine. Her next question added to my sense of unease, 'Do you know it is an offence?' I laughed nervously. Then I had to fill in my occupation. I coughed in an embarrassing way and wrote 'Bishop' and didn't know what to write in the space marked employer.

Thought for the Day

God outlives the '-isms'

—————————————

On Saturday I joined in celebrating a friend's 50 years as a priest—1936–1986. He began in the same year I was born. It made me think of all the amazing happenings of those 50 years. A *second* world war, just twenty years after wiping out a generation in the *first*, the extermination of six million Jews, the splitting of the elemental substance of the earth at Hiroshima. Any liberal humanist idea that the human race was going to proceed by education and science towards a happy and just world lay in ruins. Then followed the slow post-war recovery and the soul of the nation, which had seemed deadened by the horrors of war, began to grow fat and believe again that we could get along very well without God. We no longer needed such a primitive and childish notion, we had the technology to build a successful future, we'd never had it so good. But the shadow of Chernobyl, the arms race, the starving poor in Africa and unemployment at home make such optimism seem hollow and naive.

In these fifty years, faith in God has taken many knocks. I remember so well my first Good Friday as a priest, twenty years ago in East London. 30,000 people went to see West Ham play football, whilst in our church nearby, twenty of us listened to the old, old story of the Cross. The cinema across the road closed for lack of customers and a bingo hall opened in its place. It felt then, as it has felt many times since, that those of us who believed in God enough to worship Him were struggling against the tide. There were logical positivists who analysed our love and faith away, sociologists and psychologists who portrayed God as a Frankenstein created by human need, there were scientists who excluded God from the universe. There were literary experts who got to work on our holy books. So many of these proper and inevitable explorations and adventures of the human mind appeared to make God less credible.

Yet now the alternatives to God seem less assured. There's heaps of hedonism and horoscopes, but hardly a coherent philosophy that compares with the ageless and profound insights of the great religions of our world.

On Sunday I was in church in Hackney Wick, where we worshipped God together—men, women and children of several races—bringing some fun, some hope and a whiff of glory into our lives—and in the beauty of holiness, in the flames of many candles, in the Word of God, in bread and wine, we saw that God outlasts all our human '-isms' and our comical self-conceit, and makes a few decades seem like just a drop in the ocean of eternity. **Thought for the Day,** 3 June 1986

Truth, not fear, will set us free

I remember with happiness a time when the Church leaders in Stepney all took off their different ecclesiastical robes and made a covenant together. There was, from the large congregation, a huge burst of applause. As though it had taken *us* professionals far too long to come to the truth of so many Christian people who weren't so carefully trained in all the reasons why we should stay apart. I believe it was the same yearning for unity which led to the great outbursts of applause which greeted the

Pope in the Anglican cathedrals during his sunny visit to the United Kingdom. He touched and tapped a frustrated longing amongst many Christian people. But even though this growing harmony is real, we still have little right to preach to society about unity. The ideal and the hope is written into the Christian faith. Not only did Jesus pray that his followers may be one but the first experience of the Christian movement was exciting in that it crossed so many barriers between human beings. A desire for unity lies at the heart of many people's faith—not just those who believe in God. There is a yearning for peace, for an end to stale old battles, and the reduction of conflict. The fear of where disunity might lead us as a world makes it an important desire for everyone, because now we could destroy the human race by our earthly arguments.

People rightly say that unity is not an end in itself because unity based on falsehood is frightening. We can see nations united behind a lie—on a smaller scale, total unity in one section of a football crowd can turn to nastiness. We are all very different—and we care passionately about things. We come to value certain truths as we see them, and will stand or fall by those truths.

But perhaps there's one lesson to be learnt from the Church's difficulties, and that is just how damaging it is when we are *afraid* of other people's truths. We seemed to have been afraid of what Darwin revealed to us, and extremely nervous about Freud's contribution to human wisdom, and we still remain mostly cold and defensive against the truths contained within other religions. To be afraid of other people's truth is to shut ourselves off from a greater possible human unity. All our fear of other people's truth seems to reach its peak when opposing politicians argue. They seem totally unable to admit that the other might have some of the truth to offer; perhaps we get the politicians we deserve. Perhaps, too, the hope in the Church is like the hope in the world, where people try to listen to each other and believe the promise of Jesus that the truth will set us free—whoever says it. **Thought for the Day,** 17 January 1983

Populism and Jesus

Some vicars have to cope with a heartbreaking weekly opinion poll. As a friend of mine used to say in a loud voice, 'I see we're playing to packed houses again'. But in many churches there *are* packed houses and it is equally important that *they* are not fooled by their own *popularity*. In my experience the church is only too ready to accept the blame for low attendance, we blame it on the vicar, on the old-fashioned services, or the new-fangled ones, on the cold in the air and the cold in the heart. But we should never make our judgements *solely* on numbers.

There is a fundamental snag in the populist approach. The faith is not invented by the consumer, nor is it an entertainment, it is about the truth, the truth that can set people free. Don't misunderstand me, I enjoy being a Christian, I want the Christian faith to be popular, and I rejoice when I see our churches full, but that is not a guarantee we have got it right, any more than the apathy of people is proof that we have got it wrong.

Imagine a poll taken outside Jerusalem in AD 30. Do you think his claim to be the Son of God is

(a) An interference in politics?

(b) Naive rubbish?

(c) The truth?

50 per cent said (a), 49 per cent said (b), and a pagan soldier said it was true.

Thought for the Day, 23 November 1988

Priests too are forgiven sinners

On Monday, the House of Lords approved a measure which, if passed by the House of Commons would, on occasion, allow divorcees or people married to divorcees to be ordained priest in the Church of England. In part of the debate broadcast yesterday, Lord Lauderdale asked if such people were the right sort to help us meditate or to counsel married couples. The Archbishop of Canterbury argued that the Christian gospel is primarily about grace, and that, whilst we must uphold the ideal of lifelong marriage, we also want to witness to the hope given by Christ to those who fall short of the ideal that they can be forgiven and renewed.

Some lay people say they want to look up to their clergy as being purer and better than they are. This can be like delegating responsibility for our own goodness, but often it is a yearning for holy leaders. The Bible, however, shows that God does not always call those with a perfect record to lead his people. Abraham lied, Moses killed a man, and the apostles were not ideal candidates for ordination—Simon the Zealot was perhaps a terrorist, James and John were greedy with ambition, and Peter, the rock on which the indestructible church was to be built, betrayed the Lord himself. St Paul was stopped in his tracks as he persecuted the Christians and stood by approving when Stephen was stoned to death.

They all seem painfully human and, in one way, that is the point! God took these human beings, restored them, forgave them and then used them as signs of grace, not signs of their own strength and goodness.

People may want clergy to be free from the hurts, stains and temptations and weakness which face everyone, but we too are forgiven sinners. For most of us priests, living a godly life is just as much of a struggle as it is for the rest of you.

In the debate, Baroness Seear said she wanted the clergy to be people she could talk to. Jesus said, he who is forgiven much loves much. Those who think they are good can be very unapproachable. When someone tells me about their weakness and sins, I often know just what they mean because I've been there myself. Then like others I go to the altar and offer up my daily mess—'just as I am without one plea, oh Lamb of God I come'. It may be disturbing, but like all Christians should, we strive to be holy, but in the end we rely on God's forgiveness, not on our own goodness.

When a priest commits a serious breach of the trust he has been given he may well have to resign. The bishops are right to exercise the discipline of the Church, but to prevent someone selected for ordination from becoming a priest because of sins long past and long forgiven, would exclude most of us from the sacred ministry. **Thought for the Day,** 5 July 1989

The Church in danger?

I've been thinking about the constant criticism of the Church in the press. 'The Church is in crisis' we are told, and there are malicious and unfounded attacks upon Church leaders and even their families—distressed vicars are good for a laugh. I realize that this is par for the course—there's no news like bad news. But there's more to it than that, so what's it all about?

Let me first state the obvious, that the Church is not a perfect company of saints. We score ridiculous own goals, get caught up in damaging conflicts, fall short of what we believe the Church should be. Some churches are as lively as a railway station waiting-room—and as cold! Most of us are only too aware of our own shortcomings, indeed, we bear many of the marks of being members of the human race.

But the Church does not depend on its own goodness or achievements for its faith—it would have disappeared centuries ago if it did. No, we depend on the goodness and beauty of God. We depend on the fact that God is faithful, not that we are. This is difficult for people who judge everything by their own success to understand. We are daily reminded of our bad bits. We come to God because in Him we have found a source of endless love. God isn't put off by our crises, our betrayals, our small-mindedness. Every morning, I can go back to God and be washed clean to start again—and the Church is made up of sinners like me. We're used to crises, and indeed we often learn to know God better through them. The press bases its judgements on its own standards—above all the number of people who go to Church, but I've known churches which have been full Sunday by Sunday, and God has difficulty finding a seat. I know other churches where there are just twenty people, where God is at the centre of things. Feel the quality, never mind the width! Every Sunday, when I've finished here, I set off for one of our churches in East London. Eight, perhaps nine Sundays out of ten I experience a prayerful, friendly, multi-racial community engaged in a beautiful act of worship of God—with a lot of fun and care thrown in. It doesn't feel like a crisis to me, but rather another new beginning.

Perhaps it's society that's in crisis. All those people who have made marriage vows before God and abandoned them, all the people who have been christened and allowed their faith to dry up. When we look at the greed, the theft, the pornography, the promiscuity, the violence and the loneliness, the inequalities in our society, the cynicism of young and old—I wonder where society is going to take its crisis.

Every day, each week, the person of faith can say, 'Lord, I've messed it up again'. Here's the impossible kneeling before the inexhaustible—and we hear in our prayers and in our worship that encouraging word which says, 'Live with it, live through it, learn from it. My strength is great enough for you. You are forgiven. So get up and get on with it.'

Good Morning Sunday, 30 November 1986

Our need for God

This year I have been enjoying longer visits to the parishes of our Area. It has been a special privilege to talk with and take communion to some very elderly Christians. I met one lady who found her faith when Victoria was still alive—she was confirmed by the Bishop of Stepney in 1904. She has wonderful stories to tell of her 95 years of living.

I have also been visiting schools. The children ask some funny questions: 'Why are you wearing that pink dress, Vicar?', or one boy, seeing me walking with my crook, asked me if I had something wrong with my leg. But they also ask rather sad questions: 'Why do you wear a cross?', and many of them don't even know the name Jesus. The children are themselves sometimes wearing a cross, but it is often just a trinket with no meaning.

It is powerful and disturbing to experience this contrast between the tested faith of the old people of God and the young who have not become aware of Christ. The process of losing touch with our Christian roots has accelerated through two world wars, and the materialism and busyness of our modern world. Religion has become for so many like a war memorial—something which happened to other people. So it passes into our cultural history, but ceases to be a living reality.

I wonder what those children are going to build their lives on? What is going to be the faith which sustains them, challenges them, comforts them? We seem to be a society which mostly believes it can live on spiritual inheritance. Apparently, large numbers of us still believe in God, but is that God just a ghost from the past? Doesn't a lot of our vague talk about God cover up our sense that we have lost Him and written Him out of our minds and our agenda?

Yet people still claim that this disappearance of God is due to teachers, clergymen and the media or someone else—but it lies fundamentally with ourselves. Our children will not even know the faith they could receive, if we do not believe and practise it. All the assemblies in the world cannot compensate for God being of no significance in our homes. Those of us for whom God is still a living and loving reality, a daily source of our hope and our forgiveness, believe we have a great treasure.

People often criticize the Church, but the Church they criticize often bears no resemblance to the Church we know and love—even with all its warts. People say that faith is irrelevant, but I have to say that, looking at the deserts of the soul, the vulnerability and despair of many people—especially the young—I wonder whether the human systems, the creeds of self-sufficiency, don't simply point to our need for God of whom we still hear distant echoes. To worship is to remind ourselves of our roots, the source of our being, our purpose in life, and to catch a vision for both our life on earth and the joy of heaven.

I don't know how people manage without it!

Thought for the Day, 29 July 1987

Hidden faithfulness

This week I took part in a radio phone-in programme. The subject for people to discuss was the Church of England. Several of the callers joined in the chorus of critics: the Church was in chaos, 'irrelevant': neither the Church nor some of its bishops believed the true faith. Some of these wounds have been inflicted by Christians themselves, but there is always the press waiting to stir the conflicts on which they feed. I wanted to give you another side to the story, which will not appear in the *People* and the *Sun*, and certainly will not make the headlines.

I have just completed a year of walking round our parishes in East London. On 90 per cent of these visits I have come home tremendously encouraged and hopeful about the Church I love. For instance, this week I was in Limehouse where the vicar, Chris, his wife Marjorie and the whole congregation look after a vast church and have to raise hundreds of thousands to restore it. But they manage also to play a full part in the local community, visit the sick and the lonely, cheer up the depressed, support the local school. They are a loving, welcoming and cheerful group of people who, like the other churches in Limehouse, keep the flag of faith flying. Though some of our congregations are small, they are larger than most other local groups, and they often have a sense of family, of belonging, in places where many families are broken and people often do not feel they belong. Most of our priests and deacons are totally dedicated to their work and give whole-hearted service. Time after time in the hospitals, in the sheltered accommodation, in unemployment projects, in playgrounds and in homes, I have become aware how much this overall care is appreciated. Like other bishops, this year I have had the privilege of confirming barristers, caretakers, nurses, ex-alcoholics, black people, white people, young and old alike, who in their adult lives have discovered the love of Christ and given themselves to him.

The numbers attending church have fallen since the war (not just in the eighties) but those who belong, mean it. I have a feeling Jesus would have approved of the saying, 'look at the quality, never mind the width'. The Church is bound by its founder to value the ugly, the disabled and the unwanted, as well as the strong, the happy and the successful. Most of our churches are trying to do what almost nobody else does, and that is to create a community of people who love God, where race and class don't matter, and where people are welcomed for what they are and not what they possess. When visitors come to church this Christmas, as I hope they will do in their millions, all this human conflict will fade away, as we journey to see Christ revealing unchanging God to us. I thank him that his Church will survive the difficulties and be there to tell the story, when the 1980s have been forgotten.

Through all the noise, the beauty and harmony of the angels will teach us again that in Bethlehem was born our Saviour who is Christ the Lord. **Good Morning Sunday,** 20 December 1987

A crow or a vulture?

On 7 September 1940, a member of the crew of a Heinkel bomber looked down through the sights of his camera at the plane below him—and beyond that to the London Docklands and the Thames. The photograph he took was recovered from German archives and a copy was given to me recently on a visit to the Isle of Dogs. That bombing raid did immense damage.

As I look at the picture, I find it ironical that the docks, which could not be finally closed by war, were closed by a battle of a different kind. Containerization seemed to pose an enormous threat to a people who had worked in the docks for generations—they faced massive redundancies in the change from manhandling to automation, a large section of the community was no longer necessary. It's not surprising that they fought a hopeless battle to keep the world they knew. The docks closed and became a wasteland. Containers came and took the business down river and out of London. The lessons of that conflict should not be lost—they were paid for at too high a price.

When discussing with the developers of Docklands how local people can share in their great potential, the main argument against the most positive proposals was that 'market forces' must be obeyed. But market forces do not have a moral direction of their own, and can lead to ever greater inequalities. The advertising image of the Docklands enterprise is a friendly crow, but the people who have lived there since 1940 and before, and all the others who have made it their home since the war, wonder whether the crow might not turn out to be a vulture in disguise. If the new houses are too expensive for them to buy, the new jobs go to commuters and the wealth created is quietly extracted, how will they benefit?

This is not just a question for East London, but rather a question for the future development of our society, as we've heard in the several interviews this morning. It is also a theological question, that is, a question about which God cares—

because machines were made for man and not man for
    machines,
because neither individuals nor communities are
    expendable,
and because left to their own devices market forces can be a
    cruel deity.

Thought for the Day, 29 November 1984

Worlds apart

A few days ago, I was asked to plant a tree in one of our schools in Bethnal Green. I had great fun putting the young fir tree in the earth, and then, with the children, stamping the soil down to make it firm. There's a cherry tree in the playground, planted twenty years ago, but the only other trees in the vicinity are in the churchyard. In spite of the grilles on the windows, the poor streets and bad housing nearby, there's a happy atmosphere in the school amongst the children of many races.

The following day, in one of those stark contrasts which are such a common feature of my life, I set off by train from Waterloo, out through Surbiton to commuter land, with all the cars and bikes in the station car parks, till I arrived at my destination in the beautiful countryside in Surrey where I was to spend most of the day with boys at a public school. It's set in the wide-open spaces, with lush playing fields and *many* lovely trees.

I talked with groups of boys on almost every subject under the sun. They were lively and interesting, and, in many ways, just like teenagers anywhere.

But I felt again what I always feel when going into such a setting—a sharp cultural shock. East London and their world seem so far apart, and I wonder how these worlds can ever meet. Many of the boys will go to university, most of them will get jobs and be able to choose their future. The school tries to help them gain some insights into lives very different from their own, but overall I feel a class is still being developed who receive, from their parents and their exclusive situation, a view of society which is seriously limited. The boys were still open-minded, but the separation of their world must make it difficult to stay that way. They were concerned about poorer people, but I wondered how long that compassion would survive the influence of stereotypes and group pressures to conform.

Although I have now lived in East London for sixteen years, I went to a public school myself. I remain grateful for a good academic education, but I am also very much aware how much I have had to *unlearn* from the process. It's so easy for the so-called privileged to patronize and never to understand what it means to be on a housing list for seven years, to have no job to look forward to, to survive from one social security cheque to another.

The children who trod in the young fir tree in Bethnal Green are equally children of God, but their reality will contain a minute amount of choice as they face their future. Christ challenges people across such an opportunity gap, and calls disciples to care and work together for a more just society. What cannot be right is for those who have a wealth of choices to develop a punitive, aggressive and judging attitude to those who have few choices or none. Jesus said that the gulf between the *uncaring* rich and the poor man at his gate was unbridgeable. There is still hope if the better-off do care. I settled in my seat in the train back to Waterloo, opened my newspaper and read about the bridges burnt or unbuilt.

Thought for the Day, 28 November 1984

'Blessed are the meek'

I've noticed that sometimes when I set out on my visits in East London, I can see all the fun and excitement—and at other times I can only see the scars. One day I see the salt-of-the-earth East Ender, the wonderful variety of people, the laughter at the newsagent, the kindness, a dad and his son setting off to watch West Ham, all the banter of the markets. Another day I notice the aggression of car drivers, the obscene graffiti, the racist insults, the boarded-up flats, and feel deafened by the police sirens and downhearted by the unemployment and the homeless people waiting for the missions to open. It can certainly be a brutal place. There have been times when I have felt nearly defeated by our combined problems, and I momentarily lose sight of all the fun and the hope. I had a time like that yesterday, but then, as so often, I was saved by my job and my faith.

I had to go to one of our churches in Hoxton to confirm Sheila. She was dressed in white and wearing a white veil. Many of her friends were there. The church was beautiful and we all sensed this moment as something special. Sheila is having her fortieth birthday party on Saturday. She has Down's Syndrome. We believe that God is able to communicate with Sheila, and the familiar gospel seemed to say it all:

Blessed are the poor in spirit—theirs is the kingdom of
    Heaven
Blessed are the meek for they shall inherit the earth
Blessed are the pure in heart for they shall see God
Blessed are the peace-makers for they shall be called
    children of God.

She made her promises with her friends and I laid hands on her and anointed her. We didn't need a sermon because Sheila was teaching us what we needed to know. After the communion we all met in the hall and we had photos in which Sheila was the star, and I saw how much love and affection she sparks in people.

It's so easy to rush past the handicapped people, hide them away. But on this lovely occasion there was an affirmation of her value to God and to us. As we listened to Jesus' words, we were not ashamed to lift up the virtues of gentleness, tenderness, kindness, respect for every soul. Yet it was not a soft or sentimental occasion, but had something of the toughness of Christ. We know that the Lord we try to follow used only the weapons of love, truth and mercy to confront the brutal sharp-edged world—in fact we were aware that he was a source of strength and power which will not be defeated. As St Paul said, disturbingly, God chose what is weak to shame the strong and turn the values of the world upside down.

Thought for the Day, 11 March 1987

A variety of gifts

I want to tell you about a woman. I'll call her Jessie—she's in her fifties. She grew up in East London. Hers is a story of endless blows to her confidence. Her father was never satisfied with her. Her school was a nightmare. From being a nervous infant, she became a nervous teenager and she thought of herself as stupid and inadequate. She left school expecting nothing except a dull part-time job. She married, and discovered after many years that she could have no children. So she arrived at her fifties convinced that she was a graceless person! Yet somehow concealed inside her was a belief in herself which had not been totally extinguished.

At this point, her church woke up to the fact that she was made in God's image. She had been a faithful worshipper, Sunday by Sunday, eyes down, afraid to speak up. But then someone saw, behind her quiet exterior, her real potential. She was asked to give a talk to a parish group. It was nerve-racking, but she survived. In fact she was then asked to address a large gathering of people. She was terrified, but she conquered her fears, made her speech and sat down to prolonged applause. She said, 'I never thought the time would come when I could do that'. It had taken her 55 years to discover the value of what she had to offer.

The parish in which Jessie lives started to become more fashionable, and terraced houses, which for years had been neglected, became absurdly expensive. One of those houses was bought by a young couple in their late twenties. They were both graduates—one a lawyer, the other a chartered accountant. They were also church-goers. They were clever, articulate and caring people. They knew their faith and wanted to become part of the local church and contribute to the community. In a way, their lives had been a story of successes—they had a drawer full of certificates and degrees and qualifications.

Although they are new to East London, they face it with confidence. They earn more in a month than Jessie earns in a year. They seemed to her to know so much, and she had a crisis of confidence. What she had to say suddenly seemed so stumbling and inane. She thought she had been kidding herself that she could break out and become someone in her own right. She was embarrassed, and began to withdraw back into her shell.

It perhaps all sounds a bit like Marje Proops—but that's because many of the people who write to Marje Proops suffer real agonies through loss of confidence. This story, however, had a happy ending. Because of their belief in God's equal love, all three had the grace to learn from each other. Jessie has all the experience of struggling against failure, quietly loving and a proven faith. The young couple are wise as well as clever, and recognize how much she has to offer them. As a result, they have formed a classless friendship which is a sign of God with us—and a saving grace in our divided society.

Thought for the Day, 28 July 1987

Faith, hope, love

People in East London sometimes get angry about the way the cameras search out the worst buildings, the poorest people. This does alert people to the deprivation, yet at the same time we are proud of the East End, its history and its richness. In all my visits to our parishes I meet up with wonderful people, who have never had very much but somehow have a special way of laughing and loving and hoping.

The opposite is also true, when I meet wealthy people, the so-called 'haves'—how dispiriting it can be! They can seem so formal, so inhibited, so much wanting to protect what they have, so full of self-importance, I feel sorry for them, they have so much yet somehow they don't know how to live.

St Paul said the three great gifts of God were faith, hope and love and therefore our lives are full or empty depending on whether we receive them. As long as we're self-satisfied we won't have faith, as long as we have everything we need, hope may become unnecessary, and when we spend a great deal of energy protecting our own interests we're probably short on love. I've been in very poor homes in East London, and even poorer in Africa, which are overflowing with faith and hope and love, and I've been in luxurious thigh-deep carpet land where there is anxiety, bitterness and self-importance. As Mary, the mother of the Lord, said in her song, 'the hungry He has satisfied with good things and the rich He has sent empty away'. Or as Jesus said in an even more difficult saying, 'Blessed are the poor, for theirs is the Kingdom of Heaven'.

Good Morning Sunday, 5 July 1987

Generosity of life

A friend said that my 'Thoughts for the Day' about East London often made her feel guilty. She recognizes that I talk about real issues, but then feels powerless to do anything. She lives in London and sees the size of the inner city problems, but feels it's all beyond her. I certainly don't want to have that effect, because there are few more disheartening states than unresolved guilt.

In fact, a sense of guilt about our affluence does not always have positive results. As with guilt of all sorts, we can react by becoming aggressive. Feeling guilty is unpleasant, irritating and can spoil our sense of well-being—so we can either try to blot out the offending sore, or punish the person who raises the question. So people try to make the poverty invisible, or find a scapegoat to punish. As Jesus said, persecuting prophets is an ancient tradition.

I've also learnt that we can indulge ourselves with our guilt. It sounds absurd, but I've been in gatherings who almost relish it. At least they've done something—they've felt guilty! And now they know they are caring people. 'Bishop, your talk has done us a power of good—it's what we need to hear'—then nothing is done. Indeed, it can deepen the lethargy, because all it communicates is the impossibility of the task.

But if these are the false responses, we also have to recognize that often a sense of guilt is necessary and healthy. We are part of a stained and compromised world. So the feeling of guilt can be the moment when we see things as they are—when we share the blame—when we begin to understand the pain of other people and take steps to do something about it. If someone says they feel guilty about their affluence, the proper question is 'what are you doing about it?' Not that many of us are called like the rich young ruler to give away everything we have—but we are certainly not helpless. There is a range of useful things we can do. Often the gifts and skills of our well-off in-comers in East London are precisely those that are missing in the local community. Legal and financial advice, a car to take out someone who's housebound, professional support for an unemployment project, victim support schemes. The list is endless, and it does not have to be patronizing or dominating. Even with the heavy demands of our busy personal agenda, it should be possible to do something and to give generously.

There is that lovely biblical word 'blessed'. It's a much bigger word than 'happy'. Blessedness is a gift of God—a freedom from self-concern, a lifting of the shroud of guilt. It occurs many times in the Bible, and promises us a beautiful reward for the love we live out:

Blessed is the person who cares for the poor and needy . . .
he shall be like rain falling on early crops, like showers
    watering the parched earth.

Generosity of life is the best antidote to guilt.

Thought for the Day, 14 October 1987

Walls come down

Since I've been back at work, I've been to three marvellous parties. It might not sound very likely, but they have all been celebrations following a church service. They somehow expressed the happiness we felt in the worship itself rather like the wedding feast after a marriage. I was struck by the fact that these parties all happened in East London, as the newspapers and television raged about the terrible happenings, the riots, the crime, the racism, the violence, we had the privilege of experiencing something special, perhaps even heavenly, in the midst of it all.

I wish I could take the television cameras into the spirit of these celebrations so that people could see how lucky we are. I hope you won't think I am complacent. We've had to close many churches, and church councils, at every level, are often very like any other councils, if you know what I mean, but I want to tell you about our hope. At our parties there have been people of many races. As well as black and white East Enders, there have been people from India and China and Africa and the West Indies. There have been children and teenagers and elderly people all mixed up together. A woman whose grandchildren live a long way away enjoying being an adopted grannie to another baby, giving mum a break. A young man whom I confirmed several years ago telling me how thrilled he was because he'd got a job. A Nigerian who came to England at the time of the Biafra tragedy working in a local hospital, another young man who has been quite severely disabled since birth studying now at a polytechnic.

We get just a hint of the way we would like society to be. What's all the more annoying is that we are not all that special, we have our rows and our off periods, but we keep looking for a community where only people matter, not what they wear, whatever colour their skin, whatever their political views, whatever their status. Why do we do it? Not just because that's the best way, but also because it's the way Jesus hoped we would live. When we do, we discover the truth of his promise that the barriers can fall down. **Good Morning Sunday**

Stereotypes

I was walking down the Commercial Road in Stepney when I saw a girl coming towards me. She was wearing a shocking-pink dress, and her hair was dyed orange and green and stuck up in spikes. I was just thinking to myself: 'Look at that! I've seen some odd birds in my time', when I glanced in a shop window and caught a glimpse of myself in the reflection. There I was, dressed in a full-length shocking-pink dress. In my bright purple cassock I was unashamedly telling the world: 'I'm a Christian and I'm proud of it'. My hair also was in a streak in a forlorn attempt to persuade myself that I'm not bald yet. I thought: 'Which of us is odd?' Her clothes and hair-style declared: 'I'm me. I'm my generation—different to yours—this is what I like—take it or leave it.' I thought: 'What a pity we'll probably never be able to meet in such a way as we could understand each other'. How rarely do we make attempts to get to know the person rather than the image.

This week I want to think about divisions in our society and how to counteract them. Stereotypes are my first target. Judging a person by what we see—and all the ideas, likes and dislikes we associate with such an image—stops us seeing the person as an individual.

Some of the cruellest words in our language are built on these external judgements—'queer', 'screw', 'Paki', 'yobbo', 'the filth', 'do-gooder'. Sometimes the stereotypes have been confirmed by sad experience, by a mugging, a wrongful arrest or hurt caused by well-meaning people. But if we hide behind the stereotypes, we evade treating the person as he or she is. Indeed, crimes can be committed against a 'type': Asian people assaulted, innocent people stopped and searched, homosexuals made to resign, good policemen treated as enemies, soldiers become explodable, political opponents become monsters, right-wingers 'fascists', left-wingers 'commies'.

Jesus seemed to have a special genius for getting behind the stereotype to the person—the hated tax-collector, the thief on the cross next to him, a despised Samaritan, a centurion soldier of the occupying forces, the prostitute, a screaming maniac—they all became individuals to Jesus. He saw through to the mystery of each individual inside the exterior. He related to them, called and accepted them. **Thought for the Day,** 11 July 1982

Nothing human is alien

London Hospital 250th Anniversary service,
St Paul's Cathedral, 9 May 1990

Two hundred and fifty years ago during the War of Jenkins's Ear in the reign of George II seven men met in the Three Feathers Tavern in Cheapside. They were friends and associates who were determined to do something for the sick and the poor to the east of the City. By their generosity of spirit they founded an Infirmary dedicated to the suffering amongst the merchant seamen and manufacturing classes. Forty-five years later the Medical School was opened, because it was recognized that training and medical experience ought to go together and the vastly growing needs required many new staff.

We come to St Paul's to give thanks for a cornucopia of love and care, of scientific advance, of heroism, of generous lives and immense medical, surgical and technological skill. It is beyond our imagining to encompass what has been achieved.

Leafing through the pages of the London Hospital's illustrated history, there are pictures of the great and the world famous, of nurses starched and embattled against dirt and disease, of the poor and the sick and the underprivileged in Hogarth's cartoons, in the pages of *Punch* and staring hopeless at the first cameras.

There is Edith Cavell who trained at the London and said in a letter before she was executed on 5 August 1915, 'Standing in view of God and eternity, I realize that patriotism is not enough; I must have no hatred or bitterness against anyone'. Or Wilfred Grenfell inspired by faith to become a medical missionary to deep-sea fishermen. Or Thomas Barnardo who, inspired by Dr Hudson Taylor's revival meetings and profoundly changed by the sufferings of the East Enders, founded his house in Stepney with the words: 'No destitute child ever refused admittance'.

But a pair of pictures which stand out for me in thinking of a theme today were the portraits placed next to each other of Sir Frederick Treves and Joseph Merrick. Sir Frederick Treves was a great person in this history, surgeon to King Edward VII, an eminent anatomist, surgeon, teacher. He sits there looking every inch the successful man. Next to him is Joseph Merrick, whom he befriended when Merrick was destitute. He sits looking away from the camera, perhaps horrified at his own gross distorted face, his hand misshapen and useless lying like a torment on his lap; 'the Elephant Man'. He reminds me of those words of Isaiah describing the servant of God: 'His form disfigured, lost all the likeness of a man; he was despised, he shrank from the sight of men, we despised him, we held him of no account, a thing from which men turn away their eyes'. Somehow Sir Frederick broke through this and persuaded the hospital to let Mr Merrick stay in a room off Bedstead Square. But this in turn pointed me to the Hospital motto which I have as my theme and my text. Please excuse the Latin pronunciation, this is a risk! I hope the author Terentius Afer doesn't turn in his grave:

Humani nihil a me alienum puto.

This has been translated: 'I am a man and all calamities that touch mankind come home to me'. But I want to offer in the image of the Elephant Man: 'I reckon nothing human as alien from me'. Whatever the appearance, whatever the illness, whatever the poverty, whatever the foreignness, whatever the ugliness, whatever the attitude, I reckon nothing human as alien from me. As with the Elephant Man who stands like Christ as a symbol of innocent suffering, it was necessary to see beyond the surface to the person, to the human identity, to the human soul within. However wonderful the technology of a hospital, there remains at the heart of the business this reverence, this identification with the human being.

It is proper that we should have read the Good Samaritan story not only because of its natural association with the London in many ways, but because it goes to the same point. It's somehow sadly symbolic of our time that our discussion of the parable has been about whether the Samaritan had money in his pocket to back up his love. But the story goes far deeper, the Levite and the Priest were the professionals chosen by Jesus as types, as symbols of people who were expected to care about the good of people, but they found the wounded man too strange, too fearful, too risky, too unclean to approach. But, says Jesus, to shock his audience, a Samaritan, despised, member of a hated sect, he it was who saw the fellow human being lying by the roadside, who touched him, who bathed his wounds and cared for him. This man was the true neighbour to the man who fell among thieves.

In this parable Christ described himself. He broke through the regulations to heal the cripple, he touched and hugged the leper, he saw in the trembling, fearful prostitute a potential disciple.

To love God with all our being leads inevitably, wonderfully, to loving our neighbour as ourselves, transcending race, class, religion.

In a sense, the Hospital is a temple where this should happen, and therefore a temple where God is truly worshipped. From it should flow healing streams which will touch people of every nation, because 'to reckon nothing human as alien from me' in this way is to obey the vision of Christ himself. I pray that in the future development of the work and witness of the London, this principle will abide. I do not believe it can be done without the love of God, because we grow too tired of people, too cynical about the possibilities in each person, we need continuously to be restored by the grace of God and daily bathed in the Sun of that Grace to heal us and renew our strength and our vision.

The Inter-Faith Network

It's one of the sobering facts about religion, that it does not always improve people. For those who have been blessed with some vision of God as love, it is a source of scandal that religion is so often the excuse for hate. We all can recognize the staring, humourless eyes of the zealot who is so convinced of his own truth that he cannot listen to others, and indeed would even like the power to destroy their vision. Because I believe with passion and commitment that Christ is my Saviour should not mean that I deny that God may be speaking through His children of other faiths. Because I believe in God the Father does not mean I have nothing to learn from the wisdom and vision of millions of Hindus who believe in God the Divine Mother. In fact, as a servant and disciple of Christ who honoured the hated Samaritan, the pagan centurion, and was himself a Jew, I am bound to live in this world with a profound respect for those who search for God in holiness and desire the truth.

Yesterday I was privileged to share in the setting-up of a national inter-faith network. Rabbi Hugo Gryn and I were co-chairmen of a gathering of Sikhs, Hindus, Muslims, Christians, Jews, Buddhists and others at which we agreed our constitution. The words of our declaration were these:

> We meet today as children of many traditions, inheritors of shared wisdom and tragic misunderstanding—with the agreed purpose and hope of encouraging the growth of relationships of respect, trust and mutual enrichment between the members of the different faith communities to which we belong.

This need for greater understanding between people of different faiths is not now something we can leave to professors or missionaries, it is an urgent item on the agenda of our society. It is so easy for us to be frightened of what is strange, and to paint distorted pictures of other faiths. I sometimes wonder how Christians would cope if people, in talking about Christianity, only referred to the Inquisition or the divisions in Northern Ireland, or our age-long persecution of the Jews. We would prefer our faith to be judged by its great eternal verities, the beauty of its saints, the wonder of its love, and above all a reverence for Christ himself. So there is a necessity for listening to the faith of others and explaining our own.

Thought for the Day, 10 March 1987

As others see us

This week I spent a fascinating day with the Inter-Faith Network. Jews, Muslims, Hindus, Sikhs, Christians and people of other faiths were talking with representatives of the press, radio and television. In the debate one point kept on appearing, 'How do other people see us and our faith?' There was great concern about the way stereotypes are so easily created and so difficult to shift.

For instance what do the majority of people imagine when Sikhs are mentioned? Perhaps to some minds it will suggest just someone wearing a turban—or replay the vivid scenes in the Golden Temple in Amritsar or the picture of a man with a sword. And what about Islam—is the first picture in the frame the Ayatollah Khomeini and his followers or perhaps Muhammad Ali? How many of us come face to face with Muslims and their faith? Our conference felt that the media, especially the press, often reinforced the stereotypes with vivid pictures and stories which do not portray an accurate image of the faith community, nor properly represent their religion.

It's easier to understand this feeling for those of us who come from a Christian background if we imagine what it would be like if our faith was constantly represented by the Christians round the world we most dislike—or if it was suggested that we were cannibals because we eat the Body and Blood of Christ.

The Jews, perhaps more than any other faith community, know what it is like to be first caricatured and misrepresented and then persecuted. Yet in theory it should be easier for Christians to understand Judaism because Jesus was a Jew and our faith grew out of theirs. It is difficult for those who don't know any Sikhs or Muslims or people of other faiths to counter in their own mind the stereotypes which are on offer. When you know a Sikh family living in your street or you meet and get to know a Muslim and count Jews and Hindus amongst your friends and colleagues—then the stereotypes and misrepresentations begin to slip away.

I am always impressed by the fact that young children don't see any problem in these differences—they play and dance and sing together in school; their problems start when they learn from older children who learn it from adults that there are niggers and wogs and Pakis and Krauts—and so on.

Jesus is honoured as a prophet in Islam, valued by Hindus, respected by peoples of many faiths. He was a person who burst through the stereotypes, the hated Samaritan became a model of the good neighbour, the leper became a person and not a victim of God's punishment, and the tax collector became an apostle. It's vital for the future of our multifaith pluralist society that we resist the false caricatures of people of other faiths and the religions they profess.

This is not just a matter of theory, but of practical living, rich in opportunity but also marked by difficulties. For children who are being brought up suspended between two worlds, that of their home and faith and that of the surrounding society—or for the teachers who spend day after day with classrooms of Christian, Buddhist, Hindu and Muslim children and try to help them come to some understanding of life which will help them hold together as adults.

We shall not solve our community relations or our education questions unless we take steps to understand each other's faith—in no way to sell our own faith short, or to approve what we believe to be wrong, but in humility to meet, to listen, to speak and to learn. **Thought for the Day,** 24 November 1988

Perverting religion

On Friday night I was privileged to share in worship in an East London synagogue. The service marked the opening of the Auschwitz Exhibition, and we were there to pray and to remember the four million who died. As we stood before the scrolls, I could see in my mind's eye all those other synagogues in the thirties, where Jewish people would have been worshipping the Lord their God in the same way. I could almost hear the screams and crashes of 9 November 1938—Kristallnacht— the night of the broken glass—when 191 synagogues were set on fire, many Jews were murdered and thousands sent to the concentration camps. My thought was, 'Why were the Christians not there to prevent it happening? Why did so few stand alongside their Jewish brothers and sisters to defend their right to worship and to live in safety and freedom? Why did the Church do so little to resist as the Jews slowly became, legally and socially, second-class citizens?' Looking at the Jews in the synagogue around me on Friday, I thought it could have been *their* faces which stared at me from the photos in the exhibition, and the truth of Auschwitz suddenly became more real, personal and disturbing.

As we sang the psalms which are theirs but which we Christians also use to pray; as we recited the commandments which we both believe; as we read their Bible which is the larger part of ours—and as we shared Shalom—Peace—I thought how strange religion is. It has the power to lead people to great holiness of life. It can bring irreconcilable people together. It can give a sense of brotherhood which crosses all national and racial boundaries. It can unveil the deepest truths—yet, with a twist, an added ingredient of human wickedness, its virtues can become vices. The search for truth can become bigotry; the pursuit of goodness becomes self-righteousness.

This twisted religion can rapidly become a most fertile ground for evil movements. We have to remember that the words 'persecution', 'inquisition', 'witch-hunts', 'sectarian war', all have the flavour of religion. Yet the love of God is one of the most transforming energies we can experience and the fact that perverted religion exists doesn't mean that we should give religion up altogether—that would be like saying that we mustn't enjoy films because pornography exists. Rather we should be duly warned about the dangers. These are lessons to be learned by Jew and Christian, by Muslim and Hindu—fanaticism has not been the prerogative of any one religion.

But I think the human race has a right to expect a new chapter from the religious people of the world. If we recognize the sovereignty of God, then why do we cause, or co-operate with, so much of the conflict and injustice of the world? Why is there such religious intolerance? Our small earth has had enough of the bad fruits of religion, and needs the good fruit for survival. We need a new vision of one humanity, where those who believe different faiths respect and accept each other, being willing to learn and not just to teach. Perhaps those of us who believe in God should begin to make that our priority. We don't have to wait for the world to change—we can begin with our neighbours; Samaritans, or whoever.

Thought for the Day, 28 February 1983

The capacity for transcendence

Oxford University Sermon, 23 April 1989

Last year in Tower Hamlets the council evicted 50 homeless Muslim families from bed and breakfast accommodation. My Roman Catholic colleague and I visited the families, or rather the fathers of the families, and listened to the problem. When I spoke I set out the supportive actions we might take. Amongst the practical steps, such as opening a church to receive them and approaches to social services, I said 'We will pray for you'. At this point there was prolonged applause because for them prayer was the most important and valued thing we could do.

Before taking part in interfaith conversations about *The Satanic Verses*, I stood with my shoes off in the centre of the great Regent's Park Mosque among men, young and old, who were making complete obeisance with their foreheads to the ground. I realized that outside public schools I almost never saw young Christian men at worship and certainly not in such a demonstrative and humble way.

I tell these stories to describe the gap between the sense of God in the Muslims around us and the apparent apathy and carelessness about God in our 'Christian' society. For the Muslim community, faith is a matter of life and death, and for many nominal Christians it is a sort of hobby, a minority interest, with hollow rituals, playing at the idea of God.

It has been only too easy for the West to appear in the media and elsewhere as morally and intellectually superior, dealing with the sort of primitive religion we grew out of nearly a century ago. Those who believe in white racial superiority used it to isolate the Muslims. The Muslims are as varied in their response to God as we would expect any international community, and they have had to face great divisions and tensions amongst themselves. Islam in Saudi Arabia, Islam in Bangladesh, is as different as the Christianity of England and Christianity in Nigeria.

But for me there has been a very different lesson, which the Fatwa, the book-burning and the fanaticism of sections of the Muslim community have obscured. It is the fundamental question about our own Christian understanding of the way things are, deep within the psyche of the West. We have corporately somehow lost the faculty for belief in an encounter with 'transcendent' God. Transcendent is a big word . . . God emerging from another dimension.

Now I find that Muslims have more respect for Christianity than some Christians do themselves. They even believe more in Jesus than many Christians do, and certainly have not lost the capacity for the transcendence, mystery and authority of God in their lives.

Immediately the warning light switches on—normally transcendence, mystery and authority are good. I remember watching a film of Hitler speaking to the young people of Germany, the hypnotic power of his oratory, the grandeur of scale, the absorption into his corporate persona, 'You are of our blood', he screamed. A middle-aged man described how in the Hitler Jugend, Hitler became his God. So transcendence can lead to possession.

So we are often faced with false alternatives. On the one hand, there is reason and common sense and on the other, revelation, either the revelation in the past or the revelation to charismatic figures in the present who have the power to command blind obedience. There are Christians, often so blind to the changes in belief already made, who want to protect a fundamentalist interpretation of sacred scripture, and there are others who must remove the sense of the otherness of God by reducing it to contemporary ideas. One group defends scripture against any further erosion, whereas the other strives to express the whole truth on the basis of the contemporary incapacity to have a concept of transcendent God.

I believe this polarity is damaging to faith, damaging to theology, damaging in society, especially to the young, and it fails to do any justice to the encounter with God, now or in the past. Revelation carries to us the sacredness of God's activity and influence in universal life, as well as giving us hints of the divine being. Reason is the activity of our God-given capacity to think, to study, to verify, to evaluate. Both are essential to our journey with and to God. Both have their *limitations* which leave us needing to wrestle with reality in faith.

Reason, common sense, is a check, a safeguard and often an endorsement of faith, but only rarely does it reach into the gut, when the adrenalin is racing, the joy or hurt overwhelming.

The marriage MOT

Silver Wedding sermon, 15 May 1988

We usually concentrate our marriage guidance on the first 25 years without giving thought to the second 25. You will note that this is the opposite to cars. For the first three years they don't need much attention at all, but from then on they have the MOT every year and when they are 25 they need daily love and care. The second 25 years are fraught with new difficulties as well as some of the old. Many of us will have seen the heart-breaking sight of our aged mother and father sniping at each other, keeping scores of wrongs, somehow unable to solve the problem of always being in each other's pockets. It was Baroness Wootton who said those sad words, 'the older you get the more you become what you are'. So, all of us marriage survivors, we should regard our Silver Wedding as the beginning of the second journey and take steps to prepare for it, not so much an MOT, more a major service. Some of the issues are the same as in the first journey, others are not.

The three causes for which matrimony was ordained won't quite do. Remember them? The creation and nurture of children, that is put first—a solemn fact. Secondly, the proper use of the God-given instinct of sexuality. Thirdly, the mutual society, help and comfort that one ought to have of another, which probably should come first for the second journey. So what are the three areas which most need attention at the major service for the second 25 years? I've settled for three boring abstract nouns—relationship, contract, individuality.

When we first get married we tend to be absorbed in each other, and then, if we are lucky, children come and make up our whole agenda for a time. It's only too easy for the couple to neglect their own relationship, hence many a midlife crisis and hundreds of thousands of divorces. But for the second journey, the children will mostly have left home, though there will be continuing love and responsibility. Nevertheless we are suddenly in each other's hands, suddenly we lose one of the main daily responsibilities of our lives, but we don't lose our need to be loved and cherished physically and emotionally. Therefore romance is even more important. Careers and busyness can squeeze out the space to be, and then when the career finishes, we can suddenly find that the relationship is like the *Mary Deare*, it's still travelling but there is no one on board. It's terrifying how people can coexist like the two people in Dennis Potter's play, *The Cream in my Coffee*—the living death. So the relationships are crucial. For the second journey we need to nourish them, develop shared interests, make time for friends.

Then the contract. This is important at every stage, especially now marriages are often carrying two jobs. In marriage guidance, husbands often used to say 'She didn't ever have my tea ready'. Justice is important. As I am writing this, Sally was doing a huge pile of ironing and I felt impelled to help her hang it out. There are all the tasks, the maintenance, the shopping, the finances. The modern European family is a complex institution, whether it's two jobs or retirement, the way of life must be fair, and seen to be fair. The patterns so easily get fixed and final. But love keeps no score of wrongs, forgiveness is the heart of the matter, so we can reassess the contract, return to the mutual society, help and comfort that the one ought to have of the other. Illness and frailty often make this more difficult.

Lastly the question of individuality. We remain individuals all our lives, we are all on our own journey, and there has to be room in a marriage for that. Michael and I have known each other for 38 years, I have photos of us at school together, then as Michael and Elizabeth's best man thirteen years later and now 25 years later still, their Silver Wedding. We have all changed, we have had new griefs and joys, new traumas, new peace. The school photograph, the wedding photographs no longer tell us who we are. So in marriage we should go on developing our individuality. Marriage should never be possession. We all have our own journey to God, the journey of our soul, our inner self. As we get older we need more energy to cope with survival, fading physical power, perhaps living with pain, so each must recognize and revere the journey that their partner, as an individual, is making, in prayer and in love. One of the great souls I have known, at 85, said 'I'm getting in a rut' and went birdwatching in the Everglades!

So marriage is dependent on love which can face anything, which has no limit to its hope, its faith and its endurance.

The most valuable legacy

One of the enjoyments of coming into the studio to do *Thought for the Day* live is the taxi ride. The drivers are full of stories and philosophy even at this hour of the morning. Recently I was brought here by one who said he was a 'heathen'. A man who says that usually has a religious background and, like many men, prays to God in secret—but just won't accept more public religion. He said he was a Jew and that before moving to Romford he had lived in Bethnal Green. He said his mother had practised her faith—she would rather go out into the street to ask a passer-by to light her fire than break her Sabbath rules.

As he said that, I could hear the strong admiration for her in his voice. He was obviously still nourished by her faith even if he didn't practise it himself. She had left him a spiritual legacy. He had got the message that, to her, God's will, as she saw it, was more important than her most basic necessity. His pride in her revealed that somehow he felt he had lost something of value. Then our conversation turned to his grown-up son. What would he hand on to him? He believed that his son had caught some of the spirit of Jewish family life—he would not be ashamed, for instance, of kissing his father in public, and was proud of his Jewish inheritance—but as the generations passed, there was no doubt that the faith had become weakened. His grandchildren would have lost all direct contact with the religion which had made their great-grandmother such a special lady.

This story expressed a very widespread experience—even those of us who want to pass on our religion to the next generation have great difficulties in doing so. It's so easy to fluctuate between trying to *tell* children what to believe, and not feeling able to say anything about God at all for fear of trapping the children into false responses. That's why most parents still prefer someone else to teach their children religion—even if they don't believe it very strongly themselves. But you can't pass on a *faith to live by* second-hand.

Our children know better than anyone whether our faith is first-hand or whether it's just an optional extra gathering dust on the bookshelf. They also know whether our lives demonstrate the faith we claim to live by.

My job has brought me into so much contact with youngsters who have received from their parents a scarred inheritance—a despair about human relationships grown out of parents tearing each other to pieces; insecurity from never knowing what's going to happen to them next day. Children who have grown up in an atmosphere of resentment—trusting no one—completely alienated—in whom the indoctrination has been complete—and they become people without faith, love or hope. Seeing these stunted youngsters has always made me ponder about the legacy we will leave our own children.

Maybe as a generation we haven't thought deep enough about what life is for, but just let it pass us by—playing it by ear—living for the moment—only facing the ultimate questions when somebody dies, or something way beyond our control opens up our minds to search for reasons and meanings. I believe it is important to hand on the beliefs of great and lasting value from the past. Indeed the riches of our faith may be the most valuable legacy there is.

Thought for the Day, 7 February 1983

Sex in perspective

Through advertising, television, videos and the printed word, we are exposed continuously to sexual images. Most often, the image is of the young man or woman, beautifully in their prime, enjoying the apparent freedom of an uninhibited, thoroughly satisfying, sexual adventure. Even if the adventure ends in disaster, divorce or violence, in some way this does not diffuse the glamour. These portraits convey two messages—first, sexual activity is extremely satisfying, and secondly, we all have a right to such satisfaction. Perhaps—as with televised football—we shall be sated by over-exposure! For most people, however, a sexual appetite is stimulated which will never be satisfied. We seem to ignore the fact that so often the media personalities, who stimulate this appetite, go from unsatisfactory relationship to unsatisfactory relationship, living the deception which is being commercially exploited. It can be sobering to see the 'celluloid' beauty ten years later in the flesh, cracked and wrinkled.

Sometimes I have sat in the home of a family where the husband has been out of work for years, and the television is on. As we talk, images of the affluent world flash before us—the Christmas gifts, the holidays in Spain, the hi-fi, stereo, video, new car of the year. The whole show is beyond his reach, it's as much as he can do to survive from one social security payment to the next, let alone consider a holiday or a computer for his children—whereas there is so much in human affection, understanding and comfort he can still offer. I think this is a parable of the experience of most people who are subjected to the propaganda that total sexual satisfaction is easily accessible. We see the images of the exciting and successful sexual encounter, but feel that in our present situation there can be no satisfaction—so a sense of frustration, loss and self-pity can be created. We may look like Laurel and Hardy, but expect to be Paul Newman and Robert Redford; we may build ourselves up to a marvellous experience, only to discover that it was just the same as last time; we may momentarily see some beauty in ourselves, yet the cold light of day shows we have more in common with Hilda Ogden than Bo Derek.

The propaganda can stimulate our sexual expectations and undermine the sexual satisfaction which real life offers us. But the propaganda does not just cause dissatisfaction, it can also persuade us to get the sexual side of our lives out of proportion. Our own personal memory bank has so many sexual images imprinted that they can become a persistent playback. This can mean that grown, adult people become like adolescents, who for a period can think of little else than their sexual fulfilment. It can become a sort of addiction, which can only be fed by more fantasies if physical satisfaction is not available. So sexuality can become, through indoctrination, the most important and incessantly demanding facet of life. **Half Way**

The taboo on tenderness

The men's liberation movement does not have the same following or energy as its counterpart. I don't even know whether it exists. Because we are waking up to the stifling attitudes and closed systems which can imprison and restrict women, the war seems to be being waged on that liberation front. But I suppose that, whilst women's liberation is the most prominent battle of the sexes, an underground war is taking place in the men's zone.

Many of us men are confused, but it's not part of the male role to admit it. We will water the garden, clean the car, storm out to the pub, escape into golf, fight back our tears, show we can go it alone, and, above all, busy ourselves in our work.

We know in our hearts that we have to change, but we try to avoid it. At forty we may be faced with the fundamental question, 'What's our life for?'—and duck away from it. If we cannot find this ability to change, we shall probably make life miserable for our wife and children, for the people we work with, and mostly for ourselves. It is as though we believe that midlife crises, like religion, are best left to women. We can find ways of side-stepping the question. We will perhaps do anything except the one thing which we ought to do; that is, get through the painful experience of inner change and find the renewed and growing self.

I remember once sitting in a discussion group of priests and crying for half an hour. After the meeting, I crept away and hid myself in my room with the shame of it. Only during the night of doubt and sorrow which followed did it dawn on me that, in weeping, I had done the only sensible and truly male thing to do. The situation called for tears. How often I have thanked God that the Man I follow is reported as having wept when necessary:

Horror and dismay came over him, and he said to them,
'My heart is ready to break with grief: stop here, and stay awake'. Then he went forward a little, threw himself on the ground, and prayed that, if it were possible, this hour might pass him by.

Mark 14.33–35

A great deal of damage has been done by the too easy use of the masculine and feminine image. For instance, if feminine means partly intuitive and gentle, then there are certainly many men who have a great deal of both. If masculine means tough and decisive, then there are certainly many women who can demonstrate both qualities. It is part of a normal midlife process for the male and the female to shake off the false stereotypes.

In talking with men, I have found a desire for tenderness and the gentler qualities which they do not feel able to admit anywhere else—not at their work, not in their social life, and, most tragically, not to their wives. There are signs of hope here, as this taboo seems to be breaking a little amongst the young, who can see a desire for peace as manly; who have no difficulty in not only changing their baby's nappy, but enjoying it, and not being ashamed to enjoy it; who have women as friends and colleagues, without needing to see them as candidates for conquest. But the taboo still causes a great deal of inward suffering, and hurts a wider circle of people than just the poor confused man in the middle. If the man can allow his own so-called feminine characteristics out into his own integrated self, he often discovers that it affects his whole way of coping with life. He will need to defeat other people less, he will look for and work for greater co-operation between colleagues, and he will discover the richness of the male–female co-operation in building the just society. If he doesn't resolve it, he may feel it necessary all the time to show how hard he is, and so need to reduce the contribution that others might make.

Men do considerable violence to themselves by refusing to allow their gentler side to emerge. Pretending to be what we are not, refusing to admit our feelings, even to ourselves, disables us. It can lead to the loss of our own real self, behind the role we believe the male should play. Of course, staying vulnerable is more costly—but not in the long run, because the sustained hypocrisy and pretence lead to a disfigured personality. **Half Way**

A positive ethic for homosexuals

Even though there remains doubt about some of the causes of a homosexual personality, there is no doubt that a substantial number of people do grow to adulthood attracted to their own sex. Homosexuality is as much part of their personality as heterosexual attraction is for the heterosexual. A young man was subjected by his Christian parents to prolonged nausea therapy to convert him to 'normality'—in the process both he, his family and his friends came to see that homosexual *was* 'normal' and natural for him. There are people who are born homosexual, there are people who become homosexual, and there are some who have homosexuality thrust upon them. They are homosexuals not by perversion of a heterosexual nature, but because their nature, given and implanted by God through the process of life, has come to be homosexual. Very few homosexuals sustain as far as midlife the idea that by some miracle they could change their orientation, and those who have tried to behave as though they were heterosexual will often give up the attempt.

The teaching of the Bible has obviously been very influential in the formation of the Christian tradition. Homosexual behaviour was commonly accepted in the Mediterranean world in which the Old and New Testaments were written, but the Jewish–Christian community took a firm stand against it, stating that the physical expression of homosexual sexuality was against the will of God.

This general condemnation has been endorsed by the use of the story of Sodom and Gomorrah. This legend has had a far-reaching effect on attitudes and is the source of the word 'sodomy', which came to mean sexual intercourse between two men. It is often wrongly believed that the physical expression of male homosexual love necessarily includes anal intercourse. In the story, the cities of Sodom and Gomorrah were destroyed by God with fire and brimstone as a punishment for their wickedness in general, but especially because the men of the city demanded sexual intercourse with Lot's two male guests. Lot was rightly horrified by this demand, but his alternative solution seems to be of highly questionable morality. He says to the men of Sodom:

Look, I have two daughters, both virgins; let me bring them
out to you; . . . but do not touch these men, because they
have come under the shelter of my roof.

Genesis 19.8

I think this shows the primitive nature of the story, which
cannot provide us with adequate moral guidance. It tells more
about the wickedness of abusing people who have come for
shelter, about the cruelty and fantasies of men, and the disastrous results of such cruelty, than it does about God and
homosexual people.

Leaving this story aside, the Bible on the whole accepts the
view that homosexual behaviour is a perversion, practised by
heterosexual people. The writers' condemnations were aimed
at people who exchanged or gave up their proper heterosexual
nature to indulge in perverted homosexual misuse of others.
The exploitation of other people of the same sex as a substitute,
or an experiment, or to express sexual domination, seems to
me to be as wrong now as it was wrong in biblical times. But
these texts do not adequately deal with our contemporary
understanding. We recognize that a minority of people are
homosexual by nature or life experience, and a heterosexual
physical relationship would be, in a way, a perversion of their
personality. For this reason, it is essential that we find a
contemporary Christian morality which takes into account this
change, and which can provide the homosexual with a positive
ethic for his or her life. **Half Way**

Midlife–crisis or opportunity?

Midlife seems to be a time when we ask ourselves 'What are
we worth?', 'Where have we got to?' We may regret the choices
we've made in the past, and begin to feel especially worthless.
Not only are we getting older and feeling it, but we also find it
difficult to see what we've really achieved. 'I'm only a house-
wife', 'I'm afraid I never went to university', 'They say you're
over the top at forty', 'Don't you think it's time to stop
pretending to yourself?' . . . The message conveyed to us over

and over again is that we've moved into a different gear, although in our heart of hearts we may still feel as though we are seventeen. I remember what a boost it was to my morale when I was made a bishop, because everyone started to say how young I was, but I knew that on the squash court I was struggling, and my friends from army days were already finishing that career and looking for jobs in civilian life. So, for many people, midlife seems to be the last chance to choose an alternative life, when regrets about lost opportunities come to a head. We either see the alternatives through a haze of rose-coloured sentiment, or feel despair about the existence to which we have descended. We look desperately for a new start, a new relationship, a new set of values and rejuvenation. The mirror tells us that we are not what we were, and its cold analysis gives substance to the fears which haunt our private thoughts.

Midlife, as its name suggests, is a sort of crossroads between one half of our life and the second—or, for some, between two-thirds and the other third. It becomes the bridge between our past and our future in a way which causes many of us to feel stress. How we cope with it will make a considerable difference to the way we experience middle age and growing old. Although it can be a crisis, it can also be an opportunity when we make a new discovery about the purpose and meaning of our lives, and face the positive potential of the remaining stage of our life-span on this earth. How we tackle it can lead us into greater maturity, and perhaps even more serene middle age, or plunge us into personal chaos which is permanently damaging, not only for us as individuals, but also for many of the people around us. **Half Way**

Grace in ageing

Good morning. This week I am considering the *in-between* periods of our lives—being adolescents, and relatively middle-aged—and today, the transition from being a senior person to being an old person. Perhaps I should explain—a senior person I describe as someone who has retained control of their life, and still exercises a great deal of freedom of action. A great lady

I know aged over 80 said in a determined voice, 'It's time I took up something new'—so she went off to America to watch birds. Some people still possess power in determining their lives.

But for different people at different times, there comes a point when the control goes and the power is reduced. Suddenly the car driver can't drive safely. The walk to the bus stop is exhausting and the wait in the cold for half an hour is nearly fatal. In so many ways the independence which has been a lifetime's habit is undermined. Simple things like digging a small patch of garden or undoing screw-top jars actually aren't possible. Action becomes limited by very basic physical weaknesses. This involves a tremendous degree of letting go and acceptance.

God has much to say in this painful transition.

We spend most of our lives trying to forget that all flesh is grass, especially our own. It flourishes like the flower of the field—and like the flower it has a time and a moment in bloom and then fades. We are creatures of the natural world, however skilfully and sometimes cruelly we technically extend our stay. But faith sees this natural life as preparation for a more beautiful life, freed from the strains and tears of the years as the butterfly is freed from the chrysalis. So the person who finds the grace and the faith to accept this has so much to give to us wild activists swept along by our own busyness. When a person is stripped of so many of the ways most of us assert ourselves, there is an opportunity to discover reflection, gentleness and love.

When I give communion in churches, there is often a moment when the vicar says, 'There's Fred'—or 'Freda'—'in the congregation who can't walk up to receive, so we go to them'. They've usually been brought there by members of the church; the family of Christian people including the elderly and being enriched by their grace because they give so much to those who help them, by their faith and the way they receive help. It requires a special grace to receive; it's so much easier to give.

Thought for the Day, 18 November 1982

Jesus' manifesto!

A leading politician once suggested that the clergy should give up politics for Lent. It's a time when Christians remember that Jesus went out into the wilderness and prayed about the role he was going to live out in Palestine. After 40 days he embarked on a very public ministry which was to take him right to the centre of his country's capital city—to the heart of the political arena in Jerusalem, where he was put to death by the occupying forces.

The difficulty about giving up political issues for Lent—which would in itself be a relief—is that we would have to give up praying as well. Concern about the special social–political issues of our day grows out of prayer. Involvement is what counts to people and lends urgency to our need to pray.

To give an example: if I pray for my children at school I ask God to care for them, that they may grow into civilized, educated Christian adults. But the Lord's commandment was to love my neighbour as myself. My neighbours in Stepney also have children, so I start praying about our schools, the pressures on staff and the children. That leads me to think about the future of the Inner London Education Authority and the effects it will have on the children in the poorer areas of London. Nor do my thoughts stop there, because I think of the schools in Namibia which I visited last October. Children there have to walk many dangerous miles to school. They cannot learn after lunch because there is no lunch, they cannot write because there are no pencils or paper. I think of children and teachers being abducted and never arriving at school at all.

So, as soon as I pray for my own children, I am into prayer about my neighbours' children and the political issues which affect their education—whether in inner London or Southern Africa.

It's not that I believe that any party political manifesto would be the same as Jesus' manifesto—nor do I believe it's the task of the clergy to use their position to score party political points—Christians who pray and read their Bibles may come to different political conclusions. But to suggest somehow that there is a part of God's world which is spiritual and another part which is political is to ghettoize religion, and de-moralize politics.

Thought for the Day, 7 March 1984

Epiphany and politics

Just before Christmas, I was invited to take part in one of those television discussions reviewing the old year. They brought together three politicians—one right-wing, one left-wing and a centre forward—and me, 'the fourth person'. I wasn't sure if I was the linesman or a spectator who had been invited to join the game. Or, to change sports, it felt rather like playing mixed doubles when you don't know where to stand. I was equally exposed to a thunderous volley from the other side of the net as I was to a blow on the back of the head from my own side. In the end I decided to play singles and see how the other three coped.

The discussion was meant to come to some wise conclusion abut 1986 and look forward to priorities for 1987. The main priority seemed to be to show that party A, B or C had been and would be right and their rivals wrong. Wisdom cannot often be discovered by such a method. Imagine three people peering at the engine of a car broken down on the motorway. In tackling the problem they have to obey three rules: (1) they must all think up different solutions! (2) their own solution must be right and admit no shade of error, (3) they must demonstrate that their rivals' ideas have no value. For instance, one party says we need lots of nuclear weapons, another says we need a few, and another says we shouldn't have any. No doubt all these views are sincerely held, but where is wisdom to be found? Wisdom is an old-fashioned word which doesn't quite fit it.

We all have to put up with a great deal of political point-scoring. I think that most politicians want to serve the community, but does the compulsion to defame rivals help? Perhaps they know the rest of us too well—they believe that the political animal lurking in every breast wants above all to defeat those who hold different views from our own. Perhaps they think we will get the politics we deserve.

This strange method of proceeding came to my mind when reading the scriptures for today, when Christians celebrate the feast of the Epiphany. Three wise men studied the stars and journeyed from the East to find the new king of the Jews, the source of all wisdom. They made the political misjudgement of asking King Herod the way. They should have known that the desire for wisdom and the desire for power are hard to mix. Herod had only one interest—to destroy his rival—so he never even saw the wonder that the wise men found. They knelt in humility before the baby, offering their gifts. Humility may not win elections, but it's certainly essential to wise men, for the fear of the Lord is the beginning of wisdom.

Thought for the Day, 6 January 1987

How much is a person worth?

This week has been full of questions of value: the businessman who is paid £1 million a year, contrasted with the geriatric ward who are desperate because they can't afford the staff and equipment to give very old limbs a little comfort. Then there was that argument about the relative cost of Cruise, Trident missiles and conventional weapons, where the figures are reckoned in billions of pounds. Again, in my visits to schools in these last few weeks I have been struck by the fact that headteachers—the front line of making good citizens—despair of recruiting enough staff, and at the same time the champagne bubbles over with the creation of Super Channel—European satellite television. I know we have to make wealth to earn our living, but as we rush on, people can become just a blur. It all makes me wonder what happens to our sense of values—when we allow the elderly and the infirm to live in pain because we cannot afford the physiotherapist.

I wonder what would happen if a small starving child was brought into our own home. It would make the stereo seem less important. It often takes some terrible event to stop us in our tracks and make us think again, but it is the teaching of true religion that we don't need to wait till we have cancer—or our car crashes—to rediscover our sense of values. We need to do that now and all the time. The counter-propaganda is so persuasive, our appetites so powerful, that our own precious satisfaction can become all that matters.

Jesus made it clear what he thought was worthwhile. He put material things in their place, by comparing what he called the treasures of the earth with the treasures of heaven. The treasures of the earth grow rusty, moth-eaten, thieves can break in and steal them—their worth is superficial and does not last. Not so with the treasures of heaven. They are eternal, no one can take them away from us, they last for ever: respect, compassion, faithfulness, justice, truth, love and so on.

But even more he taught the importance of valuing people—especially those at the bottom of the heap. For him it was the leper, the prostitute, the beggar, the cripple—for in each of them he saw a child of God, distorted and battered by life. For us this is a profound challenge. How do we treat our elderly infirm, our handicapped, our mentally sick, our homeless, people with AIDS? At least we've moved on from the work-house, Bedlam, from slavery and child labour. But it's so easy for society to slip back and forget the hard-won advances we have made in the valuing of people.

Before God, the handicapped child, and indeed the handi-capped adult, are as valuable to God as the millionaire—maybe more. So when we ask 'how much is a person worth?', the answer cannot be found in a Swiss bank account or a takeover bid, but in the heart, where eternal treasures are stored.

Good Morning Sunday, 1 February 1987

Extending the family

A marriage thrives on its capacity to look beyond itself. A couple who grow into old age without thinking much of anyone else but themselves and their children are a warning sign. When all the carpets have been replaced, every possible alteration and extension made to the house, all the worn-out things discarded in favour of the new or the antique, the television is turned on—and then where are they heading? If the home and the family have become the only expression of the partnership, eventually it will lead to a vacuum. There has to be an outgoing, unselfish expression of the marriage, if it is to be whole.

A married couple who simply concentrate on themselves—their home, their family, their leisure—are basically spending their lives in self-service. I would claim that this is not only bad for individual partners, but also bad for the marriage and bad for society. For those who follow this way, it becomes increasingly necessary to protect their own standard of living at all costs. They learn to live in their own narrow world, their own comfortable home, and play no part in the vocation we all have to work for the betterment of society, or care for its members. The world we live in is full of suffering, both in the poorer nations and also in the poor and damaged of our own villages, towns and cities. People suffer just around the corner, as well as in the starvation belt.

Not only is there desperate suffering to be tackled, but also there is a necessary struggle to mend the profound damage done by evil and to work for a better world. It has certainly not been proved that increased affluence in a nation makes for less crime and less personal hurt! The violence and the lack of direction amongst young people reflect attitudes of society which they see demonstrated before them. We cannot isolate football hooliganism, thieving, sexual abuse, the drug culture, from the family and the family culture which we have allowed to become the norm. We often speak of the damage done by broken marriages, which can indeed be a huge factor in any moral disintegration of the children involved—but I believe it must also be said that much of the amorality comes from the basic selfishness of many marriages and much of our family life. So often the middle-aged people condemn our young for what is only the logical extension of our own self-centred priorities and agendas. This can be rampant materialism, or a gross self-service which leaves children, as they grow towards adult life, without any sense of service to the community or to the poor, to the damaged or to the lonely. It can also leave them with their need for idealism so frustrated that they have to find their satisfaction in other ways to fill up the great spiritual vacuum they have inherited. Jesus said:

Where your treasure is, there will your heart be also.

Matthew 6.21

Half Way

Priests against promiscuity!

It's not difficult to see why people are reacting so strongly against the 'permissive society'. To learn of people destroying their lives by promiscuity, to witness the breakdown of so many families and to hear daily of rapes, robberies and attacks on old people, gives our society a nightmare quality. The brave new world can look pretty lost and damaged. But it's important we get the analysis of the causes of all this social dis-ease right, otherwise our reactions may make things worse. For example, it's commonly said that parents should be stricter—yet some of the most rebellious and lawless children I have known have been reacting against an inflexible and strict upbringing, as well as those who have been spoilt by having no discipline at all. If we are to correct permissiveness, we have to understand it accurately.

A permissive central theme which appealed to us as a release from earlier repressive attitudes was the advice 'Be yourself'. I still believe this is part of the Christian gospel, but it begs—and has always begged—several questions, and these I think are still the questions we have to examine if we are to find a positive way forward. How does my being myself affect the capacity of the other people around me to be themselves? The commandment 'Love your neighbour as yourself' immediately puts limits on what's permitted in proper self-expression. As St Paul said, 'You, my friends, were called to be free people. Do not turn your freedom into licence for your lower nature, but be servants to one another in love.'

In my twenty years as a priest and bishop, this has not been an easy path to follow or to teach. It has felt as though we had as much chance of stemming the tide as King Canute. I was angry when I saw the Church being blamed for the permissive society, when I, like many parish priests, have constantly had to run the gauntlet of being thought of as naive and narrow-minded for trying to stand for the importance of fidelity, the value of marriage and the dangers of promiscuity. I remember in the sixties and seventies trying to put across to scornful students the Christian belief that sex should only be an expression of lasting relationships, not something for casual self-gratification. I'll never forget those wedding interviews when I struggled to introduce a Christian view of marriage to people who had been sleeping together for years, or had had several partners. Many of us have spent a large part of our lives trying to repair the broken marriages of our parishioners. In all that time, I have never heard a preacher or a Church report have one word to say in favour of promiscuity. It's not true that we haven't been preaching love and fidelity through Christ, and it's time the message was heard.

Thought for the Day, 7 January 1987

The servant's authority

When a fifteen-year-old boy tells his father to 'get lost', or when police and pickets confront each other, or when a bishop pronounces on the Christian faith, there is a common under-lying issue which affects the whole of our lives—our homes, our jobs, and the government of our country. It is the issue of *authority*. Churches have divided over it, politicians have been exiled through it, husbands and wives row about it. The bad exercise of authority and infantile responses to it produce many of our major conflicts. It fouls up our society so often, and yet we rarely hear what people think about authority itself.

There's a story of the clergyman who admonished his son, 'Remember what St Paul said, "Children obey your parents—for it is right you should honour your father and mother"'. The son replied, 'Read the next verse, Dad—"You fathers must not goad your children to resentment"'. The boy was right—there's more than one side to this authority issue. The parent who says 'Do it, because I tell you to' may have been driven to it, but will have to recognize that as the children grow more self-reliant and mature, just being a parent is not enough and will not ensure a safe majority in the house. We have to show why we think it's right, to give reasons and listen to the youngster's point of view. The parent–child approach can often be seen in our adult world of work, in our churches and in politics. When people in authority treat those under them as though they were children, a whole range of conflicts follow—because they feel they are not trusted, they see their own ideas disregarded, and the authority reinforced by sanctions and threats. Strangely enough, when authority figures dominate they ultimately undermine authority. Jesus rejected domination as his model of authority. He said to his own followers, 'I call you *servants* no longer, a *servant* does not know what his Master is about—I have called you friends'. Friends are not dominated, but respected and expected to respond in an adult way.

The timid child looks at the frightening world and hides behind its parents. Perhaps it shouldn't surprise us that, facing the *same* world, there are adults too who prefer to be dominated. They feel safer if someone else takes the responsibility. One of the pictures in the Bible most liable to misinterpretation is that of 'the sheep'. It works when the prophet says 'all we like sheep have gone astray', and it's helpful to speak of Christ as the Good Shepherd. But it does not fit Christ's call to the individual. A shepherd relies on the sheep following their leaders without question, even if they are leading them into the pen marked 'To the Slaughterhouse'. Farmers find it much more difficult to control the family's pet lambs because they develop a sense of individuality and become dissidents in the flock. Conformity can be highly attractive, and an excellent sedative on both sides of the authority fence.

If it's true that authority figures carry the parent-to-child attitude into the adult world, it is also true that many of us fail to grow out of the child-to-parent response. I must admit I have found both these childish reactions tempting. To be the sheep who safely follows my leaders, or to be the rebel who does not take into account the real consequences of my proposals. As a bishop, I find both attitudes to my own authority tricky to handle—the sheep-like because it does not challenge me and therefore leaves me carrying the whole can, and the irresponsible who doesn't actually have to carry out the decisions. But even here, I think the initiative has to lie with those in authority. Jesus acted out another startling parable when he said, 'You know that in the world, the recognized leaders lord it over their subjects and their great men make them feel the weight of authority—but I am among you as one who serves'. To press the point home, he took a towel and a basin of water, knelt before his followers and washed their feet. He joined authority and service—he was not interested in person power. No wonder the rulers of this world crucified him.

Authority was the hallmark of Jesus. The people said he

spoke with authority, not like religious leaders of his day. When he was asked whose authority he represented he said he spoke for God, he represented his heavenly Father. Most of us would hesitate before we made such a claim. When people wield authority, it's wise to ask 'Whose authority do they represent?' Are they speaking as an individual, or are they speaking on behalf of others? What right do they have to speak for others? In our social life and democracy that's a key question.

If, for instance, 18 per cent of a borough's electorate vote in an Euro-election, how far can that Euro MP be said to represent the people of the borough? If five lorry-drivers are interviewed at the blockade of a port, how far can they speak for *all* lorry-drivers? Or again, what happens if a person is a chosen representative and during their time of office they change their mind? How far do they truly represent the people—therefore how far should their words continue to carry authority?

It seems to me this is a whole area in which enormous dishonesty can operate, and which is one of the important underlying problems of authority today. If I represent certain people but they *want* and believe something very different from me, what do I do with that clash of loyalty? Do I ignore it? Where should I take a stand? As we listen to the political debate, don't we sometimes wonder where on earth the truth lies? How can they be true to all the people they represent, with so many divisions in the community, with pollsters testing opinion every week? How difficult it must be to keep integrity—to support *that* group, but not to offend another—to state the argument firmly enough for A without being too weak for C. Yet this is the sort of turmoil in which authority usually has to be exercised. This is where authority and truth have to come together—and often at considerable personal cost. The health of our community depends upon it.

Thought for the Day, 17, 18, 19 July 1984

A social anaesthetic

Last week I met three mums. They told me about their teenage children. One had a daughter who was shy and lacking in confidence—she was frightened of people really; another had a son who was full of life, attractive and popular—who fancied himself; and the third mother said her son had been unable to cope with the death of his father. All three mothers were near despair. They were living a nightmare. They had watched the moral and personal disintegration of their children. One had even had to lock her son out of home for his own good. The reason for all this is that these young lives have nearly been destroyed by their addiction to heroin. It cost them as much as £50 a day to sustain the habit, and it's so easy to get the drug if you can get the money. The mums described the addiction as the work of the devil. Certainly whatever hell might be, the drug pushers will be among the first to qualify.

I used to think that most youngsters took heroin for kicks—one of these three did. But the other two were more typical in that they took the drug to deaden the pain of life.

The hard-pressed director of a rehabilitation unit told me that the drugs were used as a sort of social anaesthetic, that is, just as heroin is administered to the dying to deaden pain, so many of these youngsters administer it to themselves because they feel they can't tolerate their past, their present or their future.

I had a chance to chat with a couple of young addicts in his unit. One, who was laying the table when I arrived, said that he was scared of going back on the streets, and that he had been thinking about Buddhism to see if it could help him. He was searching for a belief which taught that each person has within themselves the power to change their own lives. He was looking for the key that would unlock his will-power and give him the strength to be free.

As a Christian I find it heartbreaking to believe, as I do, that faith in God is the greatest possible personal power, and yet see the agonies of the young, struggling to live without it. So many of the questions they ask about their lives seem to me to be religious questions. In the face of endless unemployment, broken marriages and broken parents, and depression, faith offers each of us a way and the gift of a power within us to tackle it.

As the psalmist said,

> I waited patiently for the Lord
> He heard my cry
> I was drowning and He brought me up out of the mire
> He set my foot upon a rock and made firm my foothold
> He has put a new song in my mouth.

There are so many young people at risk, I pray they will find a rock to stand on and will sing a new song.

Thought for the Day, 27 November 1984

A covetous community

'You shall not covet your neighbour's house, your neighbour's wife, his slave, his slave girl, his ox, his ass or anything that belongs to him.' We mustn't let ourselves off the hook by denying that we've ever coveted our neighbour's slave girls or his ox, or even his ass, but what about his position in the department, his detached house, that new car?

The word 'covet' itself is not all that easy either, it's not exactly in common use. Yet this commandment, though expressed in ancient terms, is just right for our generation. It is bang on target. To covet means 'greedily desiring what belongs to someone else' or seeing what someone else possesses and passionately wanting to possess it or one like it. Let's contemplate for a moment when we last coveted. Did we watch television last night? Did we covet the life of the beautiful young couple and their beautiful child with their wonderful washing-up liquid? Perhaps not, but how can we be sure that quietly we're not being persuaded to give up coveting the Joneses' life-style and getting hooked on the Scandinavians'? I would wager, if I was a gambling man, that many of us looked at a colour supplement on Sunday. 'Those new towels could glamorize the bathroom, and even me.' 'That set of 45 saucepans would transform our culinary life.' And what about those circulars which tell us that we alone, No. 10,436, have been chosen to join in the grand draw that would enable us to buy books till death hopefully gives us an address to which not even those circulars could be forwarded?

We are a covetous community. Never before in history can a generation have been subjected to such a bombardment, a massive propaganda for the most flagrant covetings. Our competition to sell has created a monster appetite which never seems to be sated. Those who have almost nothing except a television set can experience coveting at a hypnotic level. Even the wealthy who are able to get everything they covet are not necessarily contented or even generous. In the Church we have congregations of well-off people who give less per head than some of our poorest parishes.

It's hardly surprising that there is so much stealing in society when our system is largely built on stimulating the desire to possess.

True religion attacks covetousness at its roots. Christ taught, like most of the great world faiths, that it is not what we own which gives us dignity as a person, it is what we are, what we believe, what we do. To covet, to desire what others possess, is to get trapped in one of the false solutions—our homes may be overflowing, but our hearts will be empty.

Thought for the Day, 8 January 1986

Free to choose

In a recent visit to a parish in Highbury, I met a group of people working through a huge pile of spectacles. They took each pair and checked that the frames and hinges and lenses were in good condition. If they were imperfect, they were broken up. If they were complete, they were sent to people living in Third World countries who wouldn't otherwise be able to get them or afford them. It is such a sensible idea—both recycling the glasses, which otherwise would lie wasted in the drawer, and also giving the group a very worthwhile job to do and plenty of companionship and fun as they work.

The last time I saw a large pile of glasses like this, I was involved in putting on the Auschwitz Exhibition in East

London. One of the most touching exhibits was a pile of spectacles, out of the hundreds of thousands recovered from the concentration camp. It seemed such a personal link with the victims of that horror. Glasses are usually a sign that someone is vulnerable. People who have bad sight depend on them for almost everything, and even those of us who only need them for reading can feel lost without them. The piles of glasses at Auschwitz seemed such a poignant sign of the nakedness of the poor people who suffered and died of starvation or in the gas chambers.

I couldn't help but compare the two piles, and think how different were the people working on them. The Auschwitz pile was a sign of wickedness, of fear and degrading cruelty—and the Highbury pile a sign of generosity, of voluntary work and hope for the improving of eyesight of people who have considerably less than we have. The one, the pickings from hell on earth—the other a using of precious resources for those who need—the contrast between the good compassionate Way and the evil destructive Way.

I was reminded of the old familiar words of Moses to the people of Israel: 'Today I offer you the choice of life and good, or death and evil'. Every choice we make leads somewhere—results in improving life or damaging it, in creating love or undermining it.

How we use our brain, our hands, our feet, our bodies, are all a matter of choice. Our words can encourage, bring laughter, reconcile people, or they can work spite, gloom and division. Our hands can comfort, heal and applaud—or punch, grab and vandalize. Our bodies can abuse and misuse others, or express tenderness, love and affection.

It's because of these millions of choices that we are free human beings—free to build and love; free to hate and hurt. And because we are free, we need the love of God to help us in our battle to choose the good. **Good Morning Sunday,** 5 April 1987

Free at last

For us perhaps it's just another Sunday—but for one man it's the day when he steps out of isolation into the public eye. Till last night we have seen no photographs of him since he was 44. We have watched him grow older through artists' impressions. He is now 71 and it's 27 years since he was imprisoned. He has been offered his freedom in the past—but on terms which would have kept his people as inferior citizens. Today Nelson Mandela will walk free in the hope that South Africa can create a new society. Everyone expects him to be able to find solutions. Like a messiah he comes to save. They say he can unite a country so long divided. But he carries such a burden, the ingrained cost of years separated from his wife, his family, his friends and colleagues—of living permanently under guard, never free to talk with, nor embrace, his children. He will be free—but the burden of prison will be exchanged for the burden of massive expectations and ever-present danger. There are many who want him to fail, the Nazis marched yesterday with the slogan 'Hang Nelson Mandela'—others will be filled with anxiety about their future—and their children's future. But the mass of people will be full of joy and hope. It's not just hope for South Africa but for the whole continent. It could be that the world and Africa will be able to turn from the hatred of apartheid towards positive action to enable the enormous problems which confront that beautiful land to be solved.

There is extreme poverty amongst black people, a political system in township and homeland riddled with injustice, there is the gigantic cost of divided families, and the devastation resulting from poor education. I wonder if he sees a way through it all? In his isolation has he been able to keep in touch with reality or will he feel like an alien? He will meet his old friends and colleagues in the African National Congress—he will see the dancing and cheering—but what will be going on in his head—behind his eyes?

Well, he has great resources as he steps out—he has the patience, courage and humour of his people, he has the power of prayer throughout the world. He has the determination and realism of Mr De Klerk and we hope his government and the people they represent. He has his own amazing self and the faith that has kept him going, and most important he has the right on his side. Mr De Klerk described him as a warm dignified friendly person—what forgiveness, what tolerance, what courtesy that represents in someone imprisoned for nearly three decades.

These are the resources he carries into his new world.

May God bless him, and perhaps we can all pray now as we listen to the hymn adopted by Black Africans:

Nkosi sikelele Afrika—God bless Africa.

Good Morning Sunday, 11 February 1990

Turbulent bishops?

I have been reading a recent biography of a great predecessor of mine—*Joost de Blank, Scourge of Apartheid*. He was a Bishop of Stepney from 1952 to 1957. I was overawed by the description of his time in Stepney, and then I came across his comments on an international conference: 'everyone present came to recognize the Church's right and obligation to enunciate those Christian principles on which alone a stable and developing society can be built'. Then yesterday on this programme, another illustrious predecessor of mine, Archbishop Trevor Huddleston, spoke with such power and clarity and depth of experience about apartheid. He spoke without fear or favour against an absolute evil. I was reminded of the words of Desmond Tutu: 'Religion is as dead without its political expression as politics is dangerous without the discipline of spiritual principles'—and George Bell, Bishop of Chichester, 1929–1954: 'The Church possesses an authority independent of the State. It is bound, because of that authority, to proclaim the realities which outlast change. It has to preach the Gospel of redemption . . . it is not the State's spiritual auxiliary with exactly the same ends as the State.'

I recently attended the enthronement of my colleague, Bishop Mark Santer, as Bishop of Birmingham. The congregation heard an inspiring sermon based on the Trinity, setting out some of the realities that outlast change, enunciating Christian principles on which a stable and developing society can be built. Yet as we opened our morning newspapers, we were amazed to see this was apparently a major attack upon the Government. Then, as so often, some papers said that he ought not to have said it.

Those of us who speak in public have to expect criticism and antagonism—a bishop whom no one disagrees with had best go back to his Bible for a refresher course—but what is intolerable—indeed dangerous—is the repeated assertion that the bishops ought not to say what they believe after profound reflection, prayer and wide experience. I agree that a bishop in a free country should not be party-political, but is it possible to speak on any of the major issues affecting our lives without ringing bells or discordance with party-political attitudes? God is not just God of the cassock, the hassock, the altar and the vestry, the candle and the stained glass. He is God of birth and life and death—creator of the world—lover of justice and mercy. We are constrained by this God whom we worship and who has promised to lead us towards the truth. What sort of Church would we have if its leaders were effectively silenced—what sort of society would we have if the gospel was censored?

Thought for the Day, 15 October 1987

Relative freedom

Yesterday there was a newspaper article headed 'The last few hours of freedom'. Freedom is a word which has become even more important to me in the last few months. I have been privileged to listen to the stories of Polish and Jewish survivors of the Nazis, and yesterday was the 50th anniversary of Hitler's coming to power. The memories of terror and imprisonment are still a nightmare from the time when the jackboot invaded the last corners of human privacy and freedom.

At the moment, too, we are all engaged in the nuclear debate, and pictures flash before us of human beings crawling around ruined cities, drenched with radiation—robbed of the freedom to touch or speak to another soul—without the freedom to eat or drink—only the freedom to suffer and to die.

These great shadows of fascist and totalitarian regimes, Juntas and international oppression of whatever political colour, and the capacity to wage nuclear war, put our ideas on freedom in perspective.

The headline, 'The last few hours of freedom', was concerned with none of these. It referred to the compulsory wearing of seat belts; a law which will irritate us for a moment, but also a law which will reduce the number of times that ambulance men have to disentangle heads and windscreens, that surgeons will have to sew faces back together again, and that doctors will have to tell mums and dads and children that their most loved person has been maimed for life. The advert supporting the new law shows a picture of a scarred face, and the caption reads 'It shouldn't be allowed to happen'. It's that word 'allowed' where people feel their freedom is infringed. It's wise to be on our guard against the erosion of individual rights. But how does the 'right' not to wear a seat belt compare with not being allowed to criticize a government, not being allowed to speak the truth as we see it—to live in a constant fear of raids on our homes, interrogations, years of solitary confinement, the undermining of citizenship?

There was a fascinating play some time ago on television about a confrontation between a senior trade union leader who had fought in the Spanish Civil War and a young trade unionist in today's world. The older man had been called in to help with a dispute. The issue was about the quality of toilet provision in a factory. The youngster was raring to get to the point of conflict, whilst the older man kept on seeing flashbacks of the desperate fight against fascism in Spain. That struggle for freedom put the right for better washrooms in perspective.

Freedom seems to me one of the most important words in our language. It's being played with as though it was just another word—a table tennis ball hit to and fro by presidents and politicians—a misused word to describe the way we assert our rights even at the risk of damaging others; a diluted word to which petty causes lay claim.

For freedom, Christ has set us free. Jesus, for Christians, is the model of the free life—a giving of himself, a loving and a hearing, without a trace of self-assertion. The freedom God allowed to man in him is profound and costly.

Thought for the Day, 31 January 1983

Poor or poor in spirit

There are those who say there are no really *poor* people in Britain today, and others will ask who are the poor anyway? When I first moved to Stepney, I was given a lift by a distinguished lady to a great civic feast in a chauffeur-driven car. She said to me, 'Of course, we're the poor nowadays— we've given it all away—and they're not a bit grateful'.

The old image of poverty—children without shoes, dressed in ragged clothes, showing scrawny little bodies—the sort of pictures we see in the East End Missions or the third world now— those are almost things of the past here in our welfare state. But the welfare state has huge holes in it and breaks down with striking regularity.

Also, poverty is related to the standard of living of our contemporaries; because we are all fed the same expectations, the same stimuli, we are exposed to the same propaganda and therefore can develop the same appetites. It is in the context of our own society, as it is, that poverty has to be assessed.

There are those who say to the Church, 'What about the poverty in the gin-and-Jaguar belt? The broken marriages, the depressing lack of community; neighbours behind high hedges; the veneer. The characters of *Dallas* are poorer—with all their wealth—than the people in *Coronation Street*.' There is some truth in that—it is the image of the Magnificat—'The rich He has sent empty away'. Misery breeds well in a luxurious setting, and the well-off cannot avoid the personal tragedies which affect us all. There are spiritual voids to be filled and self-assertions to be punctured, and the task of the Church in such areas, where it often looks at its strongest, can be daunting, because self-sufficiency and comprehensive insurance are hard nuts for God to crack.

Yet my experience in the inner city and in large housing estates endorses the view that there are many poor people in Britain today, who are poor not because of the way they have made their own decisions or exercised their own freedom. There are many statistics to support this belief, but for me the most convincing evidence is the people themselves. The broken old man who comes to our door almost every day for a cup of tea. The pensioner who lives alone, unfriended, in a tower block where the lifts keep on breaking down. The single mum of three children who has always been in debt and struggles from crisis to crisis. The eighteen-year-old multi-handicapped child with the mind of a two-year-old who had to move from the hospital which has been his home to an adult institution because the staff have admitted that he's over sixteen, and there's no one to save him from the system.

The most charitable thing I can say to those who assert there are no poor is that they are overprotected or blind. Ignorance is no defence in a human court of law; God may be more understanding. The Church is called to express Christ's love for the poor—God's bias—not *just* to see it in terms of financial resources, but to be committed to the regeneration of people and their environment—to work to create a chance of an abundant life for everyone, especially for those crippled by forces beyond their control. **Thought for the Day,** 10 January 1983

Dangerous success

The spiritual dangers of success, and the power which goes with it, are great and, in the long run, a far more serious threat to the soul. In accountancy, in the army, and in the Church, I have seen far too much of the personal degeneration which can accompany success to embrace it wholeheartedly as an uncomplicated friend. It is always a remarkable and memorable experience to meet the successful, powerful person who has somehow retained or learnt the humility which is the proper expression of all God's children here on earth. The necessity to win battles, the control over other people's lives, the seductive applause, the arrogance of life-style, the external protection against the small indignities, the growing conviction that we are right, and the necessity to subdue opposition—all these things can lead to a loss of inwardness, and a creation of distance between the successful person and others. Processions, rituals, childish hierarchical squabbles and the more heavily armed struggle of boardroom or staff politics, develop an armour which is both a display of strength and force, and at the same time is covering up the slightest hint of weakness or failure. City dinners, committees, politics, power games, reveal the seduction of what is called, by those who are tiring of it, the rat race. The success, the power, can all become a sort of complicated, but all-consuming projection of the self—the huge picture we have on the wall of the adult world, for everyone to see and admire and recognize. Slowly, without noticing, that external expression of the self becomes so important that the soul is given in its service. **Half Way**

The cycle of hate

At school I was a *fat* boy. I remember a biology class when the others were having an academic discussion about whether Thompson would survive longer if shipwrecked in the freezing Atlantic than more normal-shaped boys. It was many years before I managed to think of that without feeling hurt. It's amazing how small details in our own personal history are remembered with bitterness—as though there is a supercharged resentment section of our memory tank.

As when a couple get into a divorce war, they develop a sad ability to recall all the hurtful things their partner has done. The prosecution is never short of a thousand instances of rejection. We all have our personal defeats, and how much they hurt can help us understand the strength of reactions of people who have experienced the greater tragedies of war.

I wonder if you saw the man interviewed in Beirut—he had just been bombed out of his house. He was holding his small boy in his arms. He said: 'Now I shall fight to the death, and I shall teach my child to do the same'. I was struck by the contrast between the tenderness with which he held his son and the venom of his words. Another brand had been burned into another family, scarred for perhaps three or four generations.

Sometimes when we see these cycles of violence we feel trapped by the past. But in some cases the injustice which caused the bad history still exists generations later. There are still dispossessed Palestinian refugees; and Israelis, who have experienced so much suffering and pain in their own story, must know that there will be no peace until there is justice in the way the land is shared.

But some history does not refer to injustice now. It is stale, and is handed on from generation to generation to keep hate alive. I'm not saying that we should forget the past. The Holocaust, the atomic bombs must be remembered as the most costly learning experience of mankind—as a warning of what we human beings can do to each other. But we long for a fresh start—that we shall be able to deal with the problem as it now is—rather than the way it has been through the centuries.

Jesus, too, was trapped by a cycle of hate in Jerusalem, but he began a process which is open to each of us—he did not hate those who hated him. He told his disciples: 'Love your enemies—pray for those who persecute you'. He launched a forgiveness programme. To Romans who oppressed his people, and even to those who whipped him and trussed him up, he said: 'Father forgive'. He saw people clearly with the hate filter removed. This is not only a difficult example for us to follow, but also a source of great hope—because we believe he showed us the essence of God Himself. **Thought for the Day,** July 1982

Jesus and the election

On Bank Holiday Monday we were in Somerset. In the lovely May weather I watched the swallows and house martins chat each other up on the telephone wires, and the collared doves coo in the fir trees, and a small boy feed Polo mints to his pony lying down in the meadow. It was all very beautiful and idyllic— but I thought it had an extra quality this time, because I had not listened to the radio, watched television, read a newspaper for *three* days—so I had heard no mention of polls, smears or own goals. Then we returned to London to find nasty little leaflets attacking opponents, misrepresenting policies, popping through our letter box. It was Sir Winston Churchill who said, 'Democracy is the worst form of government—except all the others!', and I like the words of the elderly lady who said, 'I never vote dear, it only encourages them!' Yet, however much we might want to hide away from the debate and go into retreat, we should not. For this is God's world and He has entrusted it to us. We in turn have to decide whom we will trust to exercise the heavy responsibility of political power. But so much electioneering seems to appeal to the worst in us. Some politicians and much of the press assume we enjoy—even admire—character assassination. Personal insults fly thick and fast—maybe we do enjoy a slanging match, but it's not good, not healthy and it certainly doesn't help us choose our MP.

There is also electioneering which treats us as though we were only interested in what's in it for *us* and suggests that our only aim in life is to be a 'consumer'. Imagine coming to the judgement of God and saying, 'Well Lord, I've been a great consumer in my life!' He will say to us, 'What have you given? What service have you done for your fellow men? Have you loved well?' 'Well Lord, I always voted in my own best interests and according to my established prejudices.'

I wonder how Jesus would react to our election? Can you see him sitting at some party rally? I think he would probably be reduced to silence. But as we listen to the talk in these next ten days, some of his words may seem very apt for those seeking to win our votes, as well as for us—on *being always right* Jesus said, 'remove the plank from your own eye then you will see to take the speck from your brother's eye'. On *personal insults* he said, 'If a person abuses his brother he must answer for it, if he sneers at him he will have to answer in the fires of hell', and on *the purpose of life* he said, 'Man shall not live by bread alone, but by every word which proceeds from the mouth of God'.

But then I don't think Jesus would win an election, because to choose him as our leader would be to turn upside down many of the values which are so popular. Yet as Christians we have to vote for the party which we believe most nearly reflects the hard but lovely manifesto which Jesus gave to those who love him, and continue to pray and live—'Thy Kingdom come, Thy will be done on earth as in heaven'.

Good Morning Sunday, 31 May 1987

109

Bomb disposal

I take as my text John chapter 15, verse 13:

> 'Greater love hath no man than this, that he lay down his life for his friends.'

It is a great honour for me to be able to speak at this celebration of thanksgiving to mark the 50th Anniversary of the formation of the Royal Engineer Bomb Disposal Section. As a Royal Tank Regiment man I appreciate the invitation! One of my closest friends was a Royal Engineer and the only lesson I've learnt about Engineers from him is never go on holiday with one! It is not possible to lie on the beach in idle bliss—there is always a project to be performed like building the twelve-foot-high sandcastle, the rock which provides a perfect course through tunnels and over bridges for golf balls to race each other down to the foot with sundry children screaming the odds, or even trying to find a way to stop the ocean coming in.

But on a more serious note, as Bishop of Stepney I hope I may speak for East Enders as a whole, who have a thousand potentially explosive reasons to be thankful to Bomb Disposal units. Our gratitude for lives and houses and streets saved rings down through 50 years. It is also appropriate that we should be gathered now in the City of London and especially in St Paul's because this great cathedral church was saved from almost certain destruction on two occasions—once when a thousand-kilogram bomb was removed by Royal Engineers—the bomb landed outside St Paul's and embedded itself deep into the ground, destroying a gas main. The bomb was armed with a long-delay fuse which may have incorporated an anti-disturbance device. There was no known 'render-safe' procedure for it at the time and the normal action was to blow up the bomb *in situ*. To do so would have severely damaged, possibly destroyed St Paul's. However, Captain Davies and Lance-Corporal Wylie managed to extract it from the ground, whilst three members of the team suffered gas poisoning, and they drove it to Hackney

Marshes (still fused), where they blew it up. They received the George Cross. Those inspiring, dramatic pictures of St Paul's standing unharmed with fires all around it, which convinced a nation at war that God would stand by them, were owed to the Bomb Disposal units.

The Sections were formed 50 years ago when it was realized that Civil Defence would not be able to cope. By the end of June 1940 there were 220 sections and by September 10,000 Royal Engineers were on bomb disposal duty throughout the UK dealing with up to 2,000 unexploded bombs at any one time. The battle to counter the enemies' fiendish devices cost very dear— 397 officers and men were killed and 209 wounded—30 received the George Cross (two posthumously), but of course the majority who risked their lives daily did not receive awards, except our eternal gratitude and their reward in heaven.

This roll of honour continues down to this day, because the unexploded bombs are still being unearthed, and in the Falklands War Staff Sergeant Prescott died while defusing a bomb on HMS *Antelope*. He was awarded the Conspicuous Gallantry Award and Captain John Phillips, then a Warrant Officer Class 1 in 33 Engineer Regiment, was seriously injured and awarded the Distinguished Service Cross. So the professional skills, developed over the years, and the outstanding bravery, go on, and there are many people here who know this in the vivid memories of many moments when you risked your lives.

We have come to God's house to thank God for all this. How are we to interpret it? There is an instinctive human response to the fear of explosion—to back away, to take shelter—here are people who, backed by immense professional skill and team-work, have to advance towards it, to turn right into it. Though no doubt they are saying to themselves, 'all we have to do is follow the procedure', they may also be asking 'What if this one is different?' 'What if there is an unexpected element?' One of the officers described it to me: 'You're sitting astride a bomb, and even when you know all the procedures, even when the bomb has been there for fifty years, your legs can still go weak'.

I want to suggest that in this act of duty and self-giving, men reflect the nature and character of God Himself as revealed to us in Christ. As he prayed in the garden of Gethsemane, 'Let this cup pass me by', as he faced up to certain death, as he looked towards Jerusalem, he knew what the risks were. He said those brave words to his disciples, 'Up, let us go forward'.

111

Instead of turning away from the sacrifice, he turned towards it—a deliberate act to save humankind. It was this sacrifice which demonstrated that God is love: not sentimental love, not erotic love, not selfish love, but self-giving love. It explains why the height of love was to lay down one's life for one's friends. In a world where we are described as 'consumers', where we are encouraged to worship ourselves, where there is greed and envy, where we think the earth is ours to mutilate, this message of the Christian faith, this word that, at the heart of our being, at the heart of creation, there is the energy of self-giving sacrifice, this is the gospel our generation needs.

In his sacrifice Jesus was drawing the sting of evil, defying it, immunizing society and individuals against the explosive wickedness beneath the surface of human behaviour, seeing the danger and facing right into it, at the risk of his life, to save mankind.

In some ways then, bomb disposal is a parable of the nature of God Himself. It is therefore a calling to all Christian people— in our own way, certainly less dangerous, but also significant— to give our lives to the service, and even saving, of others, in the love of aged and ailing parents, in the love of the lonely and the homeless, in the service of our children, our friends. St Paul puts it like this:

> I beseech you brothers and sisters, by the mercies of God, that you present your bodies, a living sacrifice, holy, accept-able to God, which is your reasonable service.

Death in a different light

We are part of nature, and we ignore this fact at our peril. Man has tried to show he is superior to the rest of nature and, because nature is so transient, he has often found it uncomfort-able to see himself as subject to its laws. Yet from the first insight that man is made from dust, the mortality of man and his inescapable place in the cycle of nature is confirmed. From the moment of the inbreathing of life till the last breath when we return to the earth, we are earthly, natural creatures. Those of us who lead funerals are often reminded of this fact by the use of Psalm 103:

> For he knows how we were made,
> he knows full well that we are dust.
> Man's days are like the grass;
> he blossoms like the flowers of the field:
> a wind passes over them, and they cease to be,
> and their place knows them no more.
>
> *Psalm* 103.14–16

This, at first sight, is a solemn reminder of our transience, but I think there can also be a deep comfort in the recognition that we are all part of the natural order. People who live close to the land, and who are much nearer to the natural cycles and rhythms, seem to treat birth and life and death in a much more accepting way. The seasons bring the wonder of new life, the blossom, the fruit, and the quiet comfort of the leaves returning to the earth and received by it. Why should it be so fearful to share the rhythm of the natural creation? What's so terrifying about it? That's the nature of the earth in which human life is possible . . .

. . . Because the Christian faith has invested so much of its teaching in the Resurrection, it is my belief that we tend to skip over the comfort of God's creation and our being part of it. It is amazing and important to me how healing it is to feel a part of nature. Maybe it is a reaction to city life, where the seasons almost pass us by, but the intense experience of the natural world is like 'coming home', a losing of self in the space and interdependent life of nature around me. Not only does it slow me down and help my body to find peace, but also it fills my whole being with what can only be described as a sort of harmony, in which for a while I know how to play my part.

There is comfort in being part of nature and accepting it, but for the person who does not believe in God, there remains the threat of the 'nothing' which lies beyond the grave. If there is no resurrection, then 'nothing' is what we would encounter— but because it is nothing, because there is no brain activity, we do not encounter it. In itself, it is not a threat—the threat is derived from the loss of all we have come to value. The fear of death, and the ultimate 'nothing' for which we are heading if there is no resurrection, is the menace of the loss of our lives. We may be persuaded of our immortality when we are young, but in midlife there are stronger hints that we are turning towards the end of life and that the pace is quickening.

For the person who believes in God, and especially for the Christian, death is viewed in a different light, because of the faith in the dimension of God. This faith cannot be delivered neatly wrapped like an insurance policy, to remove completely the anxiety caused by the fear of death, but it is a revelation which can put the journey of our body through this life's cycle into perspective. I have found it an enormous encouragement to meet such a faith in those who have nearly reached the end of their own pilgrimage, and who have hope, humour and trust about the world to come. **Half Way**

The eternal backdrop

There is a picture in the Manchester Art Gallery called the *Funeral of a Viking*. It shows a warrior lying in state on his ship as it is fired and launched ablaze out to sea. By fire and water he was entering Valhalla, the hall of the slain. It is a dramatic image of the final journey; such a contrast with the pale rituals of today's clinical and hurried dispatches.

I wonder if the Viking had a vision of Valhalla, whether, as he fought his battles, he believed he had an eternal destiny—so whether he lived or died there was a glory. Christ's Resurrection brought about an explosion of hints and visions of the glory to come. He opened the gate of heaven. This eternal scenario had a profound effect upon the way people lived their earthly lives, as St Paul put it, 'I reckon that the sufferings we now endure bear no comparison with the splendour that is in store for us'. For twenty centuries Christians lived with vibrant pictures of eternity, their chosen way would lead them to the wonder of heaven with God, or the torment of hell without Him. The martyrs braved the flames because of their certain entry into paradise. But somehow through the vast tide of secularism and two horrendous wars the eternal scene has been blotted out. So the journey from womb to brain death is widely believed to be the whole story of man.

No Valhalla, no Hades, no Elysian Fields, no angels and

archangels. We peer through a spyhole, gaining small comfort from accounts of near-death experiences, but mostly just living for today and tomorrow, with hardly a glance beyond the grave. This has been a profound change in the human psyche. It is not surprising that so many think 'Eat, drink and be merry for tomorrow we die'. For most people in our generation, heaven and the final judgement have ceased to be real. Some theologians say we must accept this state of the twentieth-century mind and discover our motivation and morality and our hope without a supernatural backdrop. But I believe that we should rebuild the eternal city, reopen our contemporary mind to a vision of the heavenly places, re-educate our imagination to the possibility of God's dimension. Perhaps our vision will not be just like the Book of Revelation, but that is no reason to close the shutter on the truth we sense but do not see. If, rather than the dead end of slipping quietly behind the crematorium curtain, we believed we entered the halls of God's glory, it would transform so much in our lives; the way we tackle terminal illness, the way we decide our values, the goals we set and the way we treat each other. **Thought for the Day,** 6 July 1989

Rebuilding paradise

Someone once described St Paul's Cathedral as an example of the three-decker universe. You looked up, into the great dome and brilliant colours of the exalted roof, to heaven; we stand on *terra firma* worshipping God on earth; and if you look through the grilles in the floor, you can see down to the crypt which must be hell, because it's so often full of clergymen talking. It was part of the power of *Honest to God*, written by Bishop John Robinson in 1963, that he pointed out to us that although we still used the language of the three-decker universe, most of us no longer really believed it. 'God "up there" and "out there"', he wrote, 'can gradually, or even quite suddenly, become meaningless or worse.' The twentieth-century mind, he said, could no longer think in three decks, and had quietly disposed of these ancient ideas which had seemed so indispensable to faith. It was a mythology which, in modern man, did not work and belonged to the past. So Ascension Day was no longer a matter of Jesus going 'up there on clouds' to sit on a great throne with God in heaven.

I believe he did us a service in that he made many of us come clean about what we were believing about God, and to many of my generation he opened in a new way the God of the deep places within ourselves—the God who was spirit, to be found by exploring the ocean of our own soul and that of our brothers and sisters. We should leave the heavenly and hellish dimensions as God's eternal secrets.

But I find that the longer I go on praying to God, the more the great pictures of the heavenly feast, the leafy glades of paradise, the throne of God, inspire my imaginings and feed my spirit. Though I don't think of it as 'up there'—or in any place— nevertheless, heaven has returned to my mind. Although I don't think of hell as 'down there', I know the taste of that empty, fearful zone where our hates and resentments and misusings of our lives are found, to blot out the light and love of God. The places are only a parable of eternity, but without such living pictures, our spirit has no mountains to climb, no reflection of the pit to which our evil is consigned. I hope that today we all may catch that sense of God in heaven, and glimpse through an opening in the wall of our material existence into the eternal city beyond.

Thought for the Day, 12 May 1988

From here to eternity

University Sermon, Edinburgh, 6 May 1990

In Crete there is a fresco from Knossos, the Minoan civilization, which shows a man being prepared for burial. He receives gifts and the first is a boat to row from earth to eternity. On Patmos nearly seventeen centuries later a man called John was exiled from Ephesus at a time of persecution and he had a vision of New Jerusalem coming down from heaven to earth with glory and a judgement. Nearly eight hundred years later a Viking warrior was buried by launching him in full armour on board his ship as it was set ablaze; by fire and water he crossed into Valhalla to the Hall of the Slain.

Over a thousand years later do we have any dream of heaven, do we possess any vision of eternity, or is the gate of heaven firmly shut? As we stand in the crematorium and listen to the canned music in a brisk, cool twelve-minute ceremony, do we truly believe that our loved one, our friend, our colleague is going through the gate of heaven or just slipping behind the curtain into the furnace to become a small urn of ashes? It is not an academic question, but one which confronts us all sooner or later, and one which the Bible tells us affects us not just after our death but now, because on this earth we can taste eternal life.

We have lost the three-decker universe, we travel through galaxies and see galaxies beyond, we have spaceship ladders with their tops in the heavens, we have a new telescope to see further and further into space, but there is no heaven up there. But we have been on a journey inwards too, we have become secular people, the creation is not the achievement of an almighty transcendent God, but a massive autonomous self-perpetuating accident, some continuing explosion, or some self-contained reality. We have been honest to God and that honesty has seen us strip away transcendent images and myths of a reality we do not see, cannot measure, cannot demonstrate, which therefore does not exist. It is as though our skull now contains our whole reality and acts like a concrete wall to prevent our dreams of heaven.

To me it is fascinating that the argument about the Virgin Birth and the Resurrection has all centred on the body. What we need above all is the belief that the tomb was empty, that the body itself was risen. We hardly seem to bother about the breakthrough of eternity into our material existence. The angels, the heavenly light, the singing of the heavenly choirs to the shepherds at his birth—what we are concerned about is whether the birth was virgin, whether the bodies of Joseph and Mary came together to create the Lord, whether the tomb was empty, the body itself defied death. This to me is a sign of our panic because we cannot cope with the eternal dimension, because we have no real belief in heaven, nor in the reality of the transcendent God. The gate of heaven for our twentieth-century minds has largely shut.

The image in Russia and Eastern Europe which has been so

evocative to me is the gold, the incense, the mystery of Orthodox liturgy, with its centuries-long struggle to keep open the gate of heaven under the grey materialism and totalitarian atheism, and shows how empty the human spirit is without God and eternity. We see it there, but we find it more difficult to see it here. Our materialism, our secularism goes so deep into our psyche that we mostly hardly notice that we have lost the eternal dimension. Our myths have become fairy stories and on the surface we do not care. Yet I believe it to be of profound importance for our psyche, for our corporate life, for the journey of our own soul.

In the West End play *Shadowlands*, C. S. Lewis is faced with the supreme test of what he had written and described in Aslan's triumphant Kingdom, what he had learnt from the Gospels and from Plato, that this earthly life is but the shadows cast by the eternal fire. *These* are the Shadowlands, and the splendour of heaven is the true reality. As his wife Joy is dying she calls out to him, 'You'd better be right, Jack'.

The writer to the Hebrews says 'Faith gives substance to our hopes and makes us certain of realities we do not see'. For me if there is no heaven there is no God, at least not a loving God. We have so many new potential parables of this eternal dimension, and maybe we shall begin to express them and rebuild heaven—with our microchips able to retain millions of pieces of information—our lasers able to penetrate an eye and heal glaucoma—with our capacity to register communication between the cells of our bodies—our technology able to pick up what the Psalmist calls the conversation between the stars. But until we rediscover the dimension of God we shall be like intellectual, spiritual, psychological moles snuffling around beneath the earth, unable to press our snouts through the soil and burst out into the beauty of the earth just out of reach, or like a butterfly trapped in a room we beat ourselves against an invisible barrier to the freedom and glory when the window is opened.

Christ on his cross looked at the man on the cross next to him and spoke of his vision for them both—'truly, my son, today you will be with me in Paradise'. Our ladder is broken, our ship is sunk, our gate is shut, so we are the new explorers with the opportunity to make the most beautiful discovery of all.

Post mortem

I was sitting in a traffic jam listening to the radio. That great actress Janet Suzman was reading an extract from a novel. One of the characters in the story said something like, 'You feel guilty because you didn't talk with her enough before she died'. 'Yes, you're right,' said her companion, 'I didn't want to.'

This snippet of conversation set my mind going along familiar paths. It took me straight back to the day my dad had the stroke which killed him. In the morning I had been talking to him and trying to persuade him to give up driving. He was an expert on cars, and had maintained his own car right up to his 80th year. Driving was a main source of his pleasure and independence, and he was very reluctant to give it up. Yet I was afraid it was dangerous, and I spoke quietly but firmly to him. It seemed ridiculous then for me—his son—to be talking to him as though he was under my control. His face was sad, though he cheered up later in the day. But that night he had his stroke.

I've often thought—I wish we hadn't had that conversation. Did I spoil his last conscious day? Did I have any right to boss him like that? Perhaps he would have had a stroke while driving—he had been ill for a long time—but the possibility of being right didn't help me, because death cuts off the conversation. Suddenly it's too late to sort out our misunderstandings, to remind us that we love each other. We realize we didn't talk enough, because we were afraid to, and so we have to live with mysteries.

This can leave us feeling guilty, almost as though we are haunted by our thoughts. We don't only have to cope with our loss, but we also blame ourselves. What can we who are left do to tackle these painful feelings?

First, we have to see that we all live imperfect lives—even in the most loving relationships, and death rarely waits for the right moment. The number of times a person has sat by a bedside for days and nights, and then finally been persuaded by the nurse to go home and get some rest—and then the 'phone rings as they reach home and they're left with a feeling they've let the person down. So we have to accept this is part of 'the tears of things'.

Secondly, I find it a help to tell my dad that I'm sorry though

119

he has died—and I don't mind saying it out loud. This is not only because I want him to know, but I also need to hear myself say it. This is where we can be such a help to each other in bereavement, that we encourage and allow each other to talk it out without making any judgements. It takes time—long beyond the time when others have forgotten.

Thirdly, we can ask forgiveness of God. I draw comfort from Peter and James and Thomas and the other disciples, who left Jesus to suffer on his own, betrayed him whom they loved so much—yet within three days there he was, restoring them, forgiving them, and bringing them peace and reconciliation.

That is the beautiful promise of God to us, too.

Good Morning Sunday, 15 February 1987

Jim Henson–creator of the Muppets

Memorial sermon, St Paul's Cathedral, 2 July 1990

This is the only memorial service where I have chuckled, driving here in the car, and had a good laugh in the vestry. I have been doing some research for this morning. To talk about the Muppets and Sesame Street is to enter a room filled with grace. I have had to try and get to know Jim Henson through the effect he and the puppets have had on people, especially children of all ages.

I think of my chat with a four-year-old I know—her eyes lit up and she immediately recited the alphabet, which ended—just to prove its source—U-V-W-X-Y-ZEE! Then she told me about all her favourite characters and, what is more, she told me about their personalities. They all seemed to reflect some part of her adventure in life. Fozzy Bear she liked because he was always trying to tell jokes which fell totally flat—he had brilliant ideas which everyone else thought were wet—but all the time he stayed loyal to his friend Kermit. She liked Oscar the Grouch, who lives in a dustbin and does not want to be thought of as good—and the Cookie Monster who dreamt that the moon was a cookie—the Heartstrongs who are totally over the top, who gushed with sublime emotion over a fish finger

120

and were plunged into grief because a friend could not come to tea. Here are the passions, the defeats and humiliation of the playground—made less frightening—less inhibiting—in perspective.

In the Muppets, behind all the troubles, the breakdown of communication, the disasters, is a loving acceptance. They may make a terrible fool of themselves but deep down they are still loved. But of course, it is not just the children who love the Muppets, it has been fun asking the clergy. A rector told me that Miss Piggy was his favourite. I have heard him use the expression '*C'est moi*, Miss Piggy' to great effect—he felt she said the things that no one else dared to say, and was not beyond using a karate chop to lend weight to her argument. This appealed to him because as a clergyman he was expected to absorb any amount of aggression, never to say anything judgemental—and there are parishioners he would like to karate chop.

In a real way Jim was a gospel writer, and many of the gospel themes appear. We humans, with all our flaws, our fears, even our bad bits, are somehow loved and redeemed. Jesus always saw through the exterior mess to an inner place where the person was acceptable to God—OK! Matthew, a tax collector, became an apostle; Zacchaeus, a little despised man up a tree, is called down to be the honoured host; the leper, rejected and untouchable, is held and seen in the light of love—in the same way Jim helped us look at ourselves in a more objective and forgiving light.

In a moment Big Bird is going to sing Kermit's song, 'It's not that easy being green—to spend each day the colour of leaves—it seems you blend in with so many ordinary things and people tend to pass you over'. But green is the colour of spring—it can be big like an ocean, or important like a mountain. The song begins with self-doubt and finishes with the words of self-affirmation, 'I am green and it'll do fine, it's beautiful and I think it's what I'll be'. To put this in a more theological way, St Paul said 'By the grace of God I am what I am'.

But perhaps above all, Jim's gift was to get on the wavelength of the world's children—to tune into the child in every adult who has not suppressed it finally and totally. This perhaps is the heart of the genius—a genius we all need. Because from the child in us come merriment, innocent loyalty, trust, loving dependence, the desire to explore and experience life, the being in touch with our feelings, the sense of wonder, the robust sense of excitement, the vulnerable concern as to how we are doing, the tender affection, the ability to love gnarled old 'grouchers', the ability to see through all the adult self-deception—'the King is in his altogether, he's altogether as naked as the day that he was born'. In all this, Jim was a gospel writer, and led us to the beautiful gate of the Kingdom of God. '"Let the children come to me—do not try to stop them, for the Kingdom of God belongs to such as these. I tell you, whoever does not accept the Kingdom of God like a child will never enter it." And he put his arms around them, laid his hands on them and blessed them.'

May the child in us find that Kingdom and enjoy it eternally, and we hear Jim's words: 'Please watch out for each other and love and forgive everybody. It's a good life, enjoy it.'